THE
HUSBAND
ON LOAN
FROM
HEAVEN

A Widow's Journey of Hope,
Healing, and Heavenly Signs

KELSY MCHENRY

The Husband on Loan from Heaven
A Widow's Journey of Hope, Healing, and Heavenly Signs
2024 - Reflek Publishing
All Rights Reserved.

Disclaimer: The purpose of this book is to encourage and inspire. The author makes no guarantees concerning the level of success you may experience by following the advice and strategies contained in this book, and you accept the risk that results will differ for each individual.

For more information: hello@kelsymchenry.com

A lyric from the following song appears on page 222:
"WAIT FOR YOU"
Words and Music by THOMAS ALEXANDER WALKER,
(CAM BLACKWOOD), (JOEL LASLETT POTT)
(c) UNIVERSAL POLYGRAM INT. PUBLISHING, INC.
ON BEHALF OF UNIVERSAL MUSIC PUBLISHING LTD.
Used by Permission- All Rights Reserved

ISBN Paperback: 978-1-962280-65-5
ISBN Hardcover: 978-1-962280-00-6
ISBN eBook: 978-1-962280-64-8

BLOOMWITHKELSY

This book is dedicated to my beloved late husband, Heath Robert Nickolas McHenry, who comes to me now in green orbs and bright rainbows, heart shapes of all kinds, colorful golf balls, and other signs sure to have been sent from above.

Heath, thank you for believing in me and in my dreams, even when I questioned myself. The unwavering love, support, and encouragement you provided me with for almost twenty-six years will carry me through my darkest days. I will always remember sitting next to you on our big, cozy round couch—your favorite spot to watch the Seattle Mariners—and typing fast and furiously on my laptop when more book ideas would come to me. You would cheer me on every time, sharing your thoughts and reminding me that writing was something I was meant to do. I just never realized that the *first* book I would write and finish would be about your untimely death.

Those precious memories, and so much more, guided me as I began the journey to becoming a best-selling published author. I wish you could be here to see the finished product because I know how proud you would be of me, and of us. Our love story will never die.

Scooby, until I see you again . . .

I love you more,

Nelly

Table of Contents

A Special Note for New Widows

Hi. I know you don't want to have this book in your hands right now. Holding a book about this deep, life-altering grief likely means you are a new widow.

Your person, the love of your life, your best friend and confidante, is no longer here. It doesn't feel fair or right or even *real*, for that matter. I know! Oh, how I know! I understand you because I *am* you. I lost my amazing husband of almost twenty-three years and the father to our three children to an unexpected accident in the spring of 2021. Nothing, and I mean nothing, can prepare you for a loss like that.

One day, your life feels pretty easy and maybe even happy-go-lucky. You're just wondering what to make for dinner. Then—*poof*—your husband is gone. Maybe without any warning at all (like mine).

And let's not sugarcoat it. No matter how hard you want to will or pray him back into earthly existence, he's not coming home. That's where it starts feeling really, *really* difficult to breathe. Am I right? It all feels so strange, like the life you knew just stopped at a dead end (literally), and you're completely numb. It's almost like you're in another dimension. Nothing makes sense, and you aren't sure how you got there.

You look around your home, tears of black mascara running down your wet cheeks, and you wonder how in the world you're going to get through the next day, let alone the next few months or years. And those huge, ugly sobs—the ones you don't recognize as your own cries? You probably never thought you could cry that hard or that often. The intense, prolonged sadness is a hollow ache in your heart so deep that you can't even describe it.

You know how sometimes in life, especially during the really dark patches, just having someone who understands what you are going through and can relate to you helps ease the pain, even just a little? I want you to know that I wrote this book so it can do that for *you*. For all of us in this uncharted territory. Our stories aren't exactly the same. Our grief will be different, and our healing journeys will take many winding paths. However, our shared widow title? Well, that basically makes us besties now. You've heard the saying "It takes a village"? Well, this kind of healing is going to take a village, and possibly a vineyard, too.

In these chapters, you will find a new friend who will be with you as you embark on this unwelcome, surreal grief journey. As women, we share so many similarities, but we also each have our own history, love stories, hopes, fears, memories, and so much more. What you and I also have in common now—which not many women share—is a unique bond. It's a bond of early widowhood that feels so heavy and raw that you don't know if you're even going to survive, let alone thrive again.

I'm here to tell you that you can survive and that you *need* to. I'll also be honest and tell you this is going to suck more than anyone will ever tell you. You are going to have to dig deep to get through these next few months. (It will be years. Let's be honest.) People will see you and say, "You're so strong." And you'll reply, "I didn't have a choice." You'll probably wish they would just shut up because you don't want to be strong. You want your husband back *right now*, and you want this all to be a nightmare that felt almost too real but was just that—a nightmare.

But unfortunately, it's not. And now we have to do the hard work. And I'm so sorry it turned out this way for you, too. We didn't choose this life. It chose us. Unless you have VIP access to the big guy upstairs (or whoever you put your faith in), neither one of us will ever get an answer to "*Why me?*" or even "*Why him?*" What we will get—and I know it's hard to see this right now—is the opportunity to learn how to grow through this grief.

Throughout these chapters, let me be that friend you can learn from and lean on as you navigate this shitty, griefy new path you never expected to walk—the one you wouldn't have chosen no matter how many times your guy left the cap off the toothpaste or the toilet seat up. Let my book be your light in the darkness when you need to feel supported by someone who understands this deep, gutting pain.

I can't take your hurt away. I really, really wish I could. But I can promise that you are capable of more than you know, even when it hurts so much. And you will survive. You will feel alive again. You will smile and laugh. And, if you want to, you will hopefully even love again. I know that doesn't seem possible. But trust me. You're not meant to be just a widow.

We're both meant for more.

Your new widow friend,

Kelsy

P.S. In some of my darkest times during this journey, all I needed was a hug or text from someone who understood. Even a virtual hug or smiley face emoji could help put me back on the right track when I was feeling derailed. I want to be that friend for you. Below is my Instagram handle. I hope you'll message me anytime you need that encouragement or an ear to listen so that I can be that friend.

Instagram: @bloomwithkelsy

Before

June 10, 1995

Who knew that standing in line for an overpriced cocktail at a crowded dance club in downtown Seattle in 1995 would be where the trajectory of my life would change overnight?

Leaning against the short black wall near the dimly lit bar, I felt like a pretty and confident twenty-six-year-old as I bounced up and down to the loud music, barely containing my excitement to be out and about. I'm somewhat of a social butterfly, and when there's something fun happening, I usually want to be part of it!

I had dressed up for the occasion—my coworker's bachelorette party—and we were having a blast. So much fun that a policeman had pulled us over earlier that evening because too many girls had been hanging out of my rolled-down car windows, singing at the top of their lungs, while I drove us to the club from the Belltown restaurant where we had started. My red Ford Probe was probably a magnet for cops. But luckily, he let us go on our merry way.

Waiting for my turn to order my drink, I glanced behind me to see who had just joined me in line. As soon as I recognized him, I felt a quick jolt of happiness to see those gorgeous blue eyes, but I couldn't help myself. As I glared at him in the sexiest way I could manage, the first words out my mouth were "F*ck you."

Startled but completely unfazed, he replied quickly with a mischievous grin and a "F*ck you, too."

I want to take you back a couple of years here. This guy, the one who ended up being *my* guy, had been in and out of my college life for some time as a simple crush. We had attended the same middle and high schools but never connected because I was older by two and a half years. We had flirted at various bars between Spokane—where we grew up—and Pullman, Washington—where I attended college. Each time we'd run into each other, we both felt something. A little spark, if you will. But we were young, having fun, and not ready for anything more.

When I look back now, that little spark reminds me of when you try to ignite a lighter and it won't stay lit. But these were brief encounters, and none would hold the flame long enough to start a fire. Prior to that fateful night standing in line together in Seattle, the last time I had seen him was a year earlier at a popular Spokane bar called Outback Jack's.

In July 1994, at the end of that summer night at Outback's and the year after he graduated from college, he ended up catching a ride home from one of my girlfriends. My best friend, Laurie, and I were there with that girlfriend that night, so I was very annoyed. I heard later that he had crashed at her house. To me, that was the ultimate betrayal—passing me over for one of my own friends. Nothing major happened between them, but my feelings were hurt nonetheless. Granted, Heath and I had never shared any deep feelings with each other, so I had absolutely no right to be upset. But I was.

I held on to that little grudge until the next time I saw him—June 10, 1995, at the club in Seattle. And then I told him exactly how I felt! Insert a big *ha ha* here because what a way to greet someone, right? And for him to say it right back? We both just started laughing, and I don't even remember what we talked about other than my warning that he had better not go home with any of my girlfriends that night!

This guy was one of the most attractive men I had ever seen or known. With the body of Adonis, crystal-clear blue eyes that swept me up in their reflection, and the quiet confidence and fearlessness of a lion, he radiated movie star status. But he was more the humble Paul Newman type, not a showy celebrity. I wouldn't have been surprised if other girls did try to pick up on him that night at the club.

After our previous few years of flirting, I couldn't help but be even more attracted to him when I saw him standing there right in front of me. He had grown into a handsome and strong young man. He wasn't the college kid I had been smitten with. And we shared such similar backgrounds that, right away, he felt like a safe connection for me.

We hung out with our friends for a while and caught up with each other. Eventually, he ended up driving me back to my apartment in my car at the end of the evening. We arrived at one in the morning, and I told him I was hungry. He then attempted to make a box of macaroni and cheese for me. I wasn't paying attention, and before we knew it, the smell of burning plastic was rolling through my small kitchen. He hadn't realized he had put the pasta pot on top of the cute ceramic lid that was meant to cover the otherwise ugly black burner. We laughed so hard, and the moment was made even funnier when he admitted he rarely cooked for himself or anyone else.

We were obviously very comfortable with each other by this point. He went to my bedroom while I was cleaning up the kitchen mess and pulled the comforter off my bed. He grabbed some couch pillows, took it all to my patio, and set up a little slumber party for us. We slept in our clothes under the stars that night. It was a sweet gesture and a simple, innocent way to end the fun but unexpected evening. This was all his idea, and I remember thinking we would probably have some pretty amazing adventures if we dated.

Somehow, our romantic flame finally ignited that night, and from that moment on, we were inseparable.

This is where our love story begins.

Summer 1995

Within the first two weeks of dating Heath after that chance meeting at the dance club, I knew he was *the one*. We just fit. We completed each other. The little spark quickly burned brighter with the more time we spent together. Growing up in the same small town and knowing so many of the same people made it easy to trust each other and feel connected. We had so much in common that we always had something to talk about. Many times, we would finish each other's sentences or fill in a story that the other couldn't remember.

My best friend's younger sister was one of Heath's closest friends growing up. My older sister was best friends with his twin aunts. His other aunt was my hair stylist in high school, and she also happened to be our favorite server when my mom treated us to dinner at the nearby steakhouse. My mom even remembers buying eggs at his grandparents' produce stand when she was a young girl. The circle was infinite, and his being from a big Greek family made it even more enjoyable and fulfilling to be part of his life. I had found my very own Greek god.

By August 1995, we had been dating for two months and wanted to be together as much as possible. Most weekday mornings, Heath would walk ten minutes to the nearby coffee stand in Green Lake and pick up our drinks while I showered and got ready for work. He'd come back and sit on the side of the bathtub, and we'd visit and enjoy our coffee while I did my hair and makeup. Those sweet little gestures—bringing me my iced mocha and just wanting to spend time with me—were what I loved about our relationship. We wanted to take care of each other in whatever ways that looked like for us. I vividly remember one fall weekend when we didn't leave my apartment for two days straight. We just enjoyed the time alone together, sharing secrets and bonding.

I realized that Heath just might be in love with me the day I received a dozen red roses from another man. My friends had given my work address to a bartender we knew who wanted to date me. They had told him I was seeing someone, but he thought it might be worth a shot. That evening after work, Heath stepped into my apartment, noticed the bouquet on my kitchen counter right away, and asked who they were from. I told him, explaining honestly, that I had been flattered by the delivery but was not interested in the guy at all. Without saying a word, he immediately walked over to the counter, pulled the red roses out of the vase, and proceeded to push them down, one by one, into my kitchen sink disposal. I was annoyed but secretly happy at the same time.

I knew he was the person I wanted to spend the rest of my life with the day we went rollerblading together one sunny Sunday afternoon in September. We had just pulled into an empty parking lot in North Seattle, and I looked over and couldn't help but notice how big and powerful his muscles looked. They were on full display because he was sporting a blue Old Navy tank top, and he looked so sexy. As he turned the car off and pulled the key out of the ignition, I caught a glimpse of a big clump of white deodorant stuck to his armpit hair. I will always remember laughing inside and thinking, *I'm going to take care of this guy. I think this is my person. I'm going to get him clear deodorant instead, and I'm going to do all the things I need to do to take care of him.*

What a random way to know you're in love, but that was it for me. I wanted to nurture him, take care of him, and grow old with him. I *knew* he was the one that day. And yes, I did buy him the clear deodorant soon after, and I told him that story months later!

In those first few months together, we spent our days off exploring the city and all it had to offer, often walking for miles and just talking for hours at a time. He took me flying in somewhat rickety little rental planes to different islands in the San Juans, but I was never nervous with him because he was such a confident and calm pilot. We camped under the stars next to little tarmacs and by cold Pacific Northwest rivers, met each other's families, road-tripped to several nearby towns, and quickly became a couple. Sometimes, we would hop in the car to head somewhere, and he would purposely find a different route, just in case we ran into something cool to do. We never lacked adventure!

Around this time, I came up with a nickname for Heath, and he loved it. But, as a financial advisor, he was also adamant that I never use it in front of his clients. You'll see why in a minute! There was a rap song out called "Scooby Snacks" by the band Fun Lovin' Criminals, and I told Heath that he was my Scooby snack. From then on, he was Scooby, and I was Nell (short for my maiden name, Nelson).

That year, for my twenty-seventh birthday, he surprised me with a cockatiel because he knew how much I love birds. George would follow us around my apartment on the carpeted floor, hopping up and down and making happy noises. When we moved in together in our own place after dating for only six months, we added a chocolate Lab puppy, Scout, to the mix. It felt like we had the beginnings of our own little family.

Our life was so good!

August 22, 1998

Three years later, after a six-month engagement, we were married in Spokane in front of two hundred and fifty of our closest family and friends. It was our very own big, fat Greek wedding. Yep, the reception was complete with shots of ouzo, kegs of beer, and Greek dancing. In true Heath style, we even went to the Greek islands for our honeymoon—my first time abroad. I was so nervous about that flight overseas. But again, Heath's quiet confidence and excitement over showing me his Greek heritage put me at ease.

It was a magical time, those three years of growing up together, renting our first home, and taking care of our dogs, Scout and Louie. We both enjoyed our work and each other, never losing that spark that had finally been lit a few years earlier.

Often, we would just look at each other and agree that we were so lucky to have each found our person. We had grown up similarly, too. Both of us were raised in Spokane Valley by single-mom schoolteachers who had been widowed very young and been left to raise their infants alone (Heath and my oldest sister, Jaimsyne). We both grew up being very close to our maternal grandparents because of that.

As a child, I didn't have what most would consider a typical family experience. My parents divorced when I was just an infant, and I spent most of my childhood at my grandparents' farm or with my mom and sisters. My mother was a single, hardworking middle-school teacher doing the best she could to raise three daughters without child support or a co-parent. I saw my dad once or twice a year when I was young, but it was not enough to build a strong bond with him or his side of the family. That didn't bother me because I didn't know what I was missing. Rather than focus on what I didn't have, I lived with the mindset that what I had was enough. I'm pretty sure I was born with my glass half full. Riding our horse, Penny, with my grandpa or helping him change the huge metal sprinklers in the pasture, eating Saturday lunches at Denny's with my mom and my grandma (Sweetie), riding my BMX bike with the boys in my cul-de-sac, visiting my sister in Los Angeles in the summers . . . those were the things that brought me joy. After graduating from college, I made a conscious effort to connect with my dad and his side of the family more, and we ended up having a nice relationship.

I look back now and am grateful to have had a happy, mostly easygoing childhood. As I got older, I did wish once in a while that I could have that "normal" family for myself. I dreamed of having a loving husband and a cozy home surrounded by the symbolic white picket fence. I worried I wouldn't find him, that I wasn't worthy because I hadn't grown up with that. I worried that maybe I wouldn't even know what to do with a love like that if I found it.

I'm so glad I was wrong because then I ran into Heath McHenry. It seemed like we were meant for each other. We weren't perfect, but we were perfect for each other.

January 2, 1999

You know how sometimes life throws water balloons at you, and other times, you just get hit with a huge, explosive bomb? Well, a catastrophic bomb dropped on us just over four months into our marriage.

It was a sunny, cool Saturday morning on January 2, 1999, in North Seattle, and Heath woke up ready for a fun ski day with his best friend, Jared. Their plan was to drive south to Crystal Mountain, about four hours roundtrip, and head back home later that night. As he was pulling on his long johns early in the morning, I started experiencing an ominous gut feeling, almost a doomsday type of emotion. It scared me enough to mention it to him, but I couldn't pinpoint what I was so worried about. It didn't stop me from wanting him to go skiing (one of his favorite activities), though, because I didn't have a clue as to why I felt that way. I just asked him to be safe, and I prayed that he would be.

That evening, Heath arrived home from his ski adventure tired, sore, and in a lot of pain near his neck and shoulders. He explained that on his last run down a steep hill, his skis had hit a patch of ice, and he'd fallen, slamming the back of his head on the hard, snow-packed ground. This was before helmets became what many skiers consider a necessity, and it was obvious he'd probably given himself a concussion. He was also quite nauseous. It clicked in my head immediately that the horrible feeling I had earlier that day had been warning me of this accident. This was also the first time I had ever felt such a premonition. It crossed my mind in the same instant that it was very eerie that this ski accident happened not long after he'd dressed up for Halloween like Sonny Bono.

You see, one of our favorite activities as a couple was hosting a Halloween bash at our home in Lake Forest Park, a quiet suburb north of Seattle. Our friends would drive from as far away as Spokane and Portland, Oregon, to join us, and we would spend days decorating our place inside and out to resemble some sort of haunted house. We loved coming up with our costume ideas, and this particular year, we decided to dress as the celebrity musical duo Sonny and Cher. Sonny Bono had been in the news a lot earlier that year because he had died in a skiing accident. I'd rented a vintage orange dress and rocked the long, black Cher wig while Heath sported a brown mustache, wig, and ski gear.

He was so creative while in character that for much of the party, he walked around on his knees to resemble the real, shorter Sonny Bono even more.

I remember saying, "Scooby, that could be bad luck, pretending to be a guy who is dead." But he simply shrugged it off and enjoyed the laughs from our guests.

The night of the accident, I urged Heath to let me drive him to a nearby urgent care so they could check him out. But he was your typical man. He would normally not want to see a doctor, but we both knew he needed medical attention immediately. So we headed out.

Hours and one rude nurse later, we were sent home with the idea that he had pulled a back muscle and likely had a concussion. He was given a prescription for muscle relaxers, but the nurse never offered X-rays of any kind, and a doctor was never brought in to confirm her diagnosis. Over the next few days, it was clear that more was going on physically with Heath than a pulled muscle and concussion.

On that Tuesday afternoon, his assistant, Eileen, called me because she was also becoming concerned about him. Heath, a skilled financial advisor, was quoting numbers incorrectly, forgetting appointments, and just not performing how he usually could. When he arrived home from work that night, he admitted he wasn't feeling well and was still in a lot of pain. He agreed to try the muscle relaxer, which he'd been avoiding since we'd picked up the prescription. He disliked taking any drugs and had been trying to ease his pain with ibuprofen and Tylenol, but they weren't doing the trick. We decided he should go see a doctor in the next couple of days.

January 6, 1999

The next morning, Heath was having a difficult time motivating himself to get to work before the stock market opened at 6:30 a.m. Usually the early bird, he was dressed in his navy-blue suit and looked great, but he just couldn't find the energy to get moving. I told him I'd call and make a doctor appointment for him to be seen as soon as possible. Then I headed out to my own job at a dental office ten minutes away. I wasn't overly concerned, figuring maybe he needed a day off to rest his body and brain after all the trauma he'd been experiencing from Saturday's incident.

An hour into my morning, he called me at work and said he felt extremely dizzy whenever he tried to stand up. He was lying down on our couch and said he could barely summon the energy to get up off of it. He was just too nauseous. I wondered out loud if maybe he had vertigo from hitting his head so hard, and he agreed that might be the problem. Since he had taken some ibuprofen on an empty stomach, I asked him to try to get to the refrigerator for a yogurt so he could have something in his system. I hung up after assuring him I'd call the doctor's office on my way back home and that I would be there shortly to pick him up. Little did I know that the life bomb I mentioned earlier was about to explode.

Pulling onto our gravel driveway in Lake Forest Park, I watched Heath walk out our front door, leaning on the white wooden railing as he made his way slowly down the stairs. He looked so handsome, but pale and exhausted. As soon as he got himself situated in my car, I immediately noticed, as did he, that he was having difficulty rolling his window down. It was a manual lever, and he just could not get his right arm to move. Within moments, he was starting to slur his words. My heart began to race as I grabbed the cell phone he had just given me for Christmas only a week earlier, and I hurriedly dialed 911. I wasn't sure what was happening, but I knew it wasn't good.

I explained what I knew about Heath's condition to the 911 dispatcher, and she asked me where the nearest hospital was. We had never needed a hospital in Seattle before, so I had no idea and began to panic a little. Meanwhile, Heath was trying to speak, trying to say something, and the operator and I both realized, although it was very muffled, that he was uttering the words *fire station*. I knew there was a fire station at the bottom of our long hill, but it was at least a five-minute drive. Fear was really kicking in for me by this time. The 911 dispatcher directed me to take him straight to the fire station, and she assured me that she would call ahead to let them know we were on the way.

I drove his Pathfinder down the winding hill as carefully as I could, worried I'd make him more nauseous than he already felt. By the time I pulled into the fire station parking lot, Heath was unconscious, with his head back against the seat, and it hit me just how critical the situation was. I waited for a long, painful minute in the driver's seat for someone to meet me outside and help us, but no one was coming. As I looked over at my beautiful husband, his ocean-blue eyes open but blank, I wasn't sure if he'd make it by the time help arrived.

Overwhelmed, and stressed that the firemen weren't outside to greet me like I expected, I jumped out of the car and bolted to their door, praying Heath wasn't dying while they took their time getting to him. The front door was locked, and I immediately began banging on the damn thing as hard as I could. I ran back to Heath's side of the car and opened it to check on him as soon as I saw that several firemen were following me with their gear.

Watching grown men carry my husband, his strong and muscular body limp in their arms, was surreal. They gently laid him on their concrete floor inside their lobby, and as soon as he was placed on his side, he began having a seizure and foaming at the mouth. Two firemen were leaning over Heath, asking him questions, and I explained the situation quickly to them so they would understand that he couldn't answer.

As I spoke with the men, I overheard another fireman a few feet away on the phone asking for a chaplain. I don't know how, but I absolutely knew what that meant as soon as I heard it. I stopped him immediately, told whoever was listening in that room that "my husband won't be dying on your floor today" in an anxious but pissed-off tone, and asked him to hang up. He explained that it was normal protocol with something urgent like this, but I stood my ground, asking why they weren't putting him in an ambulance and getting him straight to a hospital.

The fireman placed the phone back on the wall, and within minutes, the ambulance that the 911 dispatcher had requested arrived to transport Heath. The paramedics explained that I wasn't allowed to ride with them in the ambulance for safety reasons, so they told me which hospital to head to. Then they left me alone in my car to wonder if that would be the last time I'd see my husband alive.

I shakily picked up my cell phone, called the home number for Heath's godbrother, Chris, and his wife who lived nearby, and explained the dire situation as fast as I could when Edie answered. She promised to have Chris meet me at the hospital, then said a prayer for us. After hanging up with her, I quickly called my work and updated them, begging my coworker and good friend who answered to pray for Heath because, as I sadly explained, "I think he might be dying."

After navigating my way to Northwest Hospital with a thrum of fear coursing through my veins, I pulled up to the ER parking lot and looked around at the empty space. There were no other cars, and I didn't see an ambulance. Worried I was at the wrong location, I parked and ran into the ER.

Not a soul was in sight. No workers. No sick people. No one, not even someone to greet me at the front desk. I peeked through the plexiglass windows at the top of the big swinging doors to the triage area and saw firemen just chatting away with a nurse. It looked like such a casual conversation that my first thought was that Heath was gone. *They couldn't be standing around just talking if someone like him was in urgent need of care, could they?* I wondered. I was confused, scared, and angry as I tried to push the doors open to no avail. I looked around, still not seeing anyone to help me nearby, then finally crawled up and over the front desk and raced down the hallway toward them.

"Did he die? Where is he? What's going on?" As soon as I got close to the group, the words tumbled out of my mouth as quickly as the tears started welling up in the corners of my eyes.

"No, no, ma'am," one of the firefighters said. "They took him for an X-ray, and they'll be right back. There's his room." He pointed, and I thanked him, then gingerly walked toward it. Knowing my husband was still alive, I felt the giant knot in my stomach loosen a little bit.

The kindest nurse was waiting in his room, and as soon as she saw me, she explained that Heath wasn't in the room because the ER doctor had requested a CT scan to look at his head and neck. She was so calm and reassuring that I immediately felt like we were in good hands. I had felt so utterly alone that morning, between the fire station and the previous hospital visit, that I was worried sick about my husband. It felt good to have someone care.

Heath was soon back in the room, able to blink on command but otherwise looking almost paralyzed, remaining motionless and quiet. I stood by the side of the gurney he lay on, whispered in his ear, and assured him he would be fine and that I loved him. While we waited for the CT results, I noticed that he had become limp on one side of his body and was still salivating, but he obviously couldn't control it. His face drooped on the left side, and the nurse placed a tube in his mouth so he wouldn't choke on his own saliva. His eyes often closed for long periods, and each time, I honestly wasn't sure if he was unconscious or about to die.

The ER doctor arrived in the room shortly after, and it was very clear from the minute he walked in that he did not think Heath would make it. He was almost nonchalant about it, unattached as some doctors can be, and I was trying to control my growing fury toward him as he explained that nothing significant was found on the CT scan. He said we would have to wait for an MRI to get better results but that we wouldn't be able to do that until later in the afternoon because other people coming to the hospital campus had previous appointments.

I was shocked. It was blatantly obvious that Heath might not make it that long, and the doctor was adamant that we would have to wait our turn. He acted like he didn't think any treatment would work, more scans or not. He made it sound like the trauma was too much for him to survive.

As soon as he left the room, I told the nurse in no uncertain terms that he was not allowed to come back in and that I would not work with him. I urged her to find a different doctor—one who might see that Heath still had a chance. Just like with the phone call an hour earlier to the chaplain at the firehouse, I was of the mindset that no one was going to tell me that my husband was as good as dead while he still had a fighting chance to live.

Heath's nurse vehemently agreed with me that there was still hope left, and she seemed as frustrated as I was. I wanted answers, *now*, and I wasn't getting any. My whole world felt like it was hanging in limbo while I just waited helplessly to see what was going to happen next. I wondered if the next doctor who walked in would take our situation seriously.

I immediately felt some relief when the nurse got a call in the room, then explained that although the ER doctor I didn't like had not seen anything worrisome on the CT scan, the technician had. On his own, the tech had called Dr. Victor Erlich, who was one of the neurologists on the campus, and explained what he saw.

It felt like two or three years instead of just two or three hours since the morning had started. Over and over, not one person had given me any idea of what might be wrong with my husband. That all changed when Dr. Erlich stepped into the room.

With his tousled salt-and-pepper curls, he resembled a younger Einstein, and his demeanor was professional but so kind. After quickly introducing himself, he put Heath's scan up on a bright screen, flipped on the light switch, and pointed to the image of Heath's neck.

"What does that look like to you?" he asked me as he took a peek over at Heath on the gurney.

"Calcification?" I replied with a shrug, being familiar with the white, cloudy buildup I was looking at only because of my job in the dental field.

"Exactly, but that would be if Heath was a seventy-year-old man. He's not. Your husband is a fit, strong twenty-seven-year-old. And what this white area actually is, is a blood clot. Because it is filling up the entire brain stem, it is prohibiting any oxygen from getting to his brain. We need to start him on a blood thinner right away to try to break it up."

A moment of pure peace passed over me as I took in his words. His confidence in his diagnosis made me realize I was finally getting some answers. I didn't pretend to understand exactly what was going on, but I knew with my whole heart that Dr. Erlich was going to try to save my husband. It was clear from the moment he greeted me. I knew I needed to stay calm and just trust the process.

Within minutes, a heparin drip was administered through Heath's IV to break up the blood clot, and it seemed to help a little at first. Within the first five minutes, the drooling slowed down, and I watched as his limp right arm stiffened a bit. I continued whispering in his ear, reassuring him he was going to be fine, and holding his hand. It didn't matter if he could hear me or not. I just needed him to know I was there.

When the drooling stopped, I felt like I could finally catch my breath for the first time in hours. It was surreal—the balancing act of praying over him with all my might while also trying to hold my shit together at the same time.

I didn't want to cause a scene. I wanted to be calm for my husband and the people caring for him so they could do their job.

As the medicine started flowing through Heath's veins, the nurse and I could see subtle changes in his appearance, as if the heparin might be doing something. We were both absolutely in awe when his blue eyes fluttered open, looked around, found me, and looked confused.

"Scooby, you're going to be okay! Don't worry . . ." I started to say in a soothing tone. But before I could get all the words out, his eyes closed again, and he began having another small seizure. This happened several times over the course of a few minutes, and each time, I could see his face droop and his arm go limp. I felt so helpless. Each time, I lost a little bit of hope that Heath was going to survive, or at least make it out of this without serious mental and physical side effects.

Forty-five minutes after we arrived at the ER, Heath's cousin, Chris—who was also his godbrother—made it to the hospital, and it felt so good to have family with me. I had been struggling to stay calm throughout the traumatic events of the morning all by myself as I advocated for my husband's care, and as soon as I saw Chris, I was able to unload all my worries on him and know that I wasn't the only one praying for a miracle.

Our Last Chance

I wish I could say everything started working in our favor. But things were actually worsening. Dr. Erlich asked Chris and me to join him in the hospital hallway, and my heart sank as we followed him.

"Kelsy," he said in a somber tone, "you might have one hour left with your husband."

My eyes grew big, and my stomach dropped to the floor as he explained that the heparin just wasn't working fast enough to dissolve the huge clot in Heath's brain stem. He then asked how long Heath had been having the symptoms that morning, trying to pinpoint how long he'd been losing oxygen and experiencing symptoms of what appeared to be a stroke. I guesstimated it had been roughly two and a half hours since he'd called me at work.

Dr. Erlich explained that there might be one more lifesaving option that could possibly help, but it had never been used before on a patient after they'd already been given the other blood thinner. It was a medication called tPA (tissue plasminogen activator). It had to be administered within three hours of the onset of symptoms, and it could be given to a patient only once in their lifetime. He said it would take the pharmacy at least twenty minutes to mix it and that we were in a very difficult situation with timing. He explained that by the time the medication kicked in, it could still be too late to save him. Or it could cause Heath to hemorrhage internally because of the other blood thinner he had already been given.

Chris and I agreed that Dr. Erlich needed to do whatever was necessary. The doctor and I watched Chris cross himself three times in the Greek Orthodox tradition and say a quiet prayer. Then he shuffled back to the waiting room. I begged Dr. Erlich to please try to save my husband. As he walked away, I leaned against the bare, white hospital wall and prayed as hard as I could. I told God that if He took Heath now, I would have nothing left of him but his last name. I prayed that He would let me keep my husband and told Him I would gladly give up having children if I could just have my husband live.

Those twenty minutes spent waiting for the tPA to arrive were excruciating, and I was starting to worry immensely about calling Heath's mom to let her know what was happening. I was afraid to tell her anything before

I knew which way it was going to go. It was making my stomach sick to even think about it.

Now might be a good time to tell you that when Heath was just one, his own father died at twenty-five. Bruce McHenry had married the love of his life, MaryLou, the year before. And only eighteen months later, he succumbed to lung cancer just days after his birthday. He was not a smoker, so the lung cancer was a very unexpected illness.

Heath had always intuitively felt that he might not live a long life, in part due to losing his dad at such a young age. I always nervously laughed it off when Heath mentioned it, ignoring the possibility so I could continue with my own rose-colored view of our future together. I obviously had blinders on. And when the trauma from the ski accident occurred, it made it all too real, too possible, that he might not survive that day. I had gone from thinking he just had a concussion to realizing a few days later that it was much worse than I could ever imagine.

As the tPA began to work on Heath's blood clot, I watched the medicine drip down the IV, and I grappled with how and when to call my beautiful and sensitive mother-in-law, MaryLou. She had already been through so much loss in her life, losing her father to a heart attack when he was only sixty-two and then losing her first cousin and best friend, George, to a car accident shortly after. I knew I needed to wait until I had more definitive answers before scaring her more than necessary, especially because Heath was her only child.

Dr. Erlich had warned us to look for signs that Heath might be hemorrhaging, so the sweet nurse and I kept a close watch on his eyes, mouth, and fingernails for signs of bleeding. As if the whole morning hadn't been nerve-racking enough, now it seemed crystal clear that we were getting close to the end. It would be either the end of Heath's life or a brand-new beginning.

I just stood next to him, staring intently at his face and his hands, praying I would not see any blood. When I pulled his lip up to check his gums and saw bright red, my heart began to race, and I could feel my palms getting sweaty. I looked at his hands, and his nail beds were turning hot pink. I peered up at the nurse, who immediately called Dr. Erlich to warn him of the changes. I can't even explain how scared I was.

This was it. I wanted off this roller coaster so badly, and I knew that if the bleeding continued, Heath would likely hemorrhage and die soon. This was our last chance, and my heart just ached and ached as I waited for what was next.

Unbelievably, in just a matter of long, drawn-out minutes, Heath opened his eyes and started trying to sit up and get comfortable. The nurse alerted Dr. Erlich, who was still in his office. Within ten minutes or so of Heath becoming conscious and trying to communicate, it felt like things were finally falling into place. It was crazy—there is no other word for it—to watch my husband moving and nodding after all the trauma he'd been through the last three hours. My heart could finally rest, and my fists could unclench. I wasn't going to lose my husband today.

Dr. Erlich arrived back to the room, and the nurses and I were giddy to learn that the heavy-duty medication was working. The doctor explained to Heath what was happening to him, and I could tell that he was listening. But I wasn't sure how much he could comprehend. He'd been through so much over the last five days, and it was impossible to know how the trauma, the medications, and the concussion were going to affect him down the road.

After smothering my husband with hugs and kisses, I realized it was time to call his mom and let her know about the situation. I felt strongly that Heath was going to be okay. My husband had always been invincible in my mind, but Dr. Erlich did remind us that we weren't 100 percent out of the woods yet. He encouraged us to be cautiously hopeful. So, I tried to remain calm and hopeful.

I picked up the phone from the wall by Heath's bed, and as I waited for the secretary at MaryLou's elementary school to put the call through to her fourth-grade classroom, I watched in utter disbelief and dismay as Heath fell unconscious again. I couldn't believe what I was seeing, but I knew I couldn't hang up now. Without telling MaryLou that he was unconscious, I gently shared with her the simplest details I could and hung up the phone, knowing she'd be on a plane from Spokane to be with her son as soon as possible.

I wasn't sure how much more I could handle. The scene in front of me kept changing without warning. Fortunately for us, Dr. Erlich wasn't ready to give up so easily. He had returned a few minutes earlier to his office to see a scheduled patient who had a severe head injury from a motorcycle accident. Heath's nurse called the doctor's front desk and quickly explained the current situation. Dr. Erlich told her to add back the heparin on top of the tPA, so she did so. When he arrived back to the room later, he explained to Chris and me that this would be a first. He even assured me in his thoughtful manner that if Heath did not survive that day, I could possibly even have his medical license revoked because this was not a medical protocol ever tried before. He smiled as he said it, and I assured him I would never do that. Then, for the third time that day, I asked him to do whatever he needed to save my husband.

As we all stood waiting, worrying, and watching to see if the heparin would begin to do its magic, like a movie in rewind, Heath woke up again. He looked around with those piercing blue eyes, and when he tried to speak, it felt like another small miracle. His speech was still somewhat slurred, but as the minutes went by, he was able to answer a few questions. Dr. Erlich explained that if we could get him through the first twenty or thirty minutes of staying conscious, he might be out of the woods.

It was the best news I had heard all morning.

Heath miraculously survived that day. There must have been a lot of angels at work to keep him here on Earth because there were so many critical moments when he was on the verge of death. An MRI later that afternoon confirmed what the CT technician and Dr. Erlich had suspected all along, and we were finally sent up to intensive care to monitor his bleeding and oxygen for the next several days.

During his stay in the ICU, Heath told me that while he had been unconscious in the ER, he had what can only be described as a near-death experience. We never called it that when we spoke of it later, but when I look back, that term seems to make the most sense now. He remembered being outside his body and watching the events unfold from above it. He saw what he thought was a doctor walking across the big campus and then watched the man start sprinting, as if he needed to get somewhere very quickly. That man ended up being Dr. Erlich. After hearing about this a few days after Heath was saved, Dr. Erlich said that was exactly what happened. He had been walking from his office to the ER and thinking about what

THE HUSBAND ON LOAN FROM HEAVEN

could have possibly happened to Heath, a trauma patient he had yet to meet. He started running when he realized what might have happened and that time was of the utmost importance.

Later, Dr. Erlich also explained that he recognized that Heath had suffered a dissection of one of his vertebral arteries. This caused a blood clot to migrate northward to his basilar artery, creating what medical professionals call the locked-in syndrome, from which a patient has a modest chance of being rescued unless the occluding clot can be broken up promptly. Since the standard treatment then for this potentially fatal syndrome was only heparin, and because Heath had already gone beyond the allowed time to receive the newer and more powerful tPA, Dr. Erlich administered heparin first. But as you read a minute ago, it had little effect. Ultimately, the tPA aided in breaking up most of the clot. But the MRI later that day confirmed there was still some remaining, so Heath was put on a three-month regimen of Coumadin, a common blood thinner.

Miraculously, his only side effects from that day (and from his fall five days prior) were a concussion, a little vertigo, and some balancing issues with his eyes. Within a few weeks, those all faded away. He had lost some weight while in the hospital and recovering at home, but he was able to get back into the gym quickly, always working toward the future and wanting to be his best self. He was the unstoppable Greek god I'd married, able to bounce back like the strong warrior we all knew him to be.

My prayers as a newly married bride were answered that morning back in 1999. God let Heath survive so we could continue to build our lives together. And, although I had told Him we'd be fine with no kids, I secretly hoped we'd still be able to grow our family and have some beautiful little McHenry babies.

February 1999

A month later, still underweight from his accident and still requiring weekly blood draws to monitor his blood thickness, Heath decided he was ready to hit the gym again. Dr. Erlich explained on a call that the damaged artery was healing on its own with no surgery necessary and would likely be stronger than ever. This was some of the best news we could hear because Heath never knew when to stop when it came to sports and working out, even when he probably should have. He wanted to make the most of his time here on Earth, especially after surviving his accident. Nothing and no one ever intimidated him. If anything, difficult situations made him work harder toward his goals.

The first time we met Dr. Erlich in his office, weeks after the accident, Heath wanted to know what he was and was not allowed to do. The doctor explained that certain activities, like scuba diving, would not be a good idea for him, and we both looked at each other, shrugged, and nodded. Neither of us had ever been interested in that, so it was not a big deal.

Then Heath asked Dr. Erlich if he could still go helicopter skiing. My blood pressure spiked as the doctor answered that he didn't think that would be an issue. Small puddles of tears welled up in the corners of my eyes as the doctor looked at me and asked if I wanted to hold my person, my husband, back from doing the activities he loved. My emotions were still so raw from the traumatic past month, but I knew what the right answer was. From then on, I had to safeguard myself from worry by wearing a protective layer of nonchalance (or naivety) that Heath would always be fine. He hadn't been taken from me that January morning, so I was sure we were safe and God wouldn't take him now. I was certain He wouldn't do that to MaryLou, either. No one should be put through as much emotional pain as she had been.

Once Heath was cleared to stop his weekly blood draw appointments, I urged him to go on a guys' trip and have fun with his two best friends, Jared and John, as soon as possible. We agreed that if we were going to start a family, we wanted to try to get pregnant sooner rather than later. I wanted him to enjoy his independence a little more before we started our family.

Six months after the accident, Heath and the boys were thrilled to plan a vacation to Greece. I was happy to see our lives getting back on track, and Heath looked as healthy and strong as ever. It was only when I started experiencing that scary fluttering deep in my belly right before his trip abroad that I began to worry about their plans.

Heath never dismissed my intuition that morning he had gone skiing and hit his head back in January, so when similar disturbing feelings started to creep up on me two weeks before his Greece trip, I tried so hard to let it go. But they wouldn't leave me alone. The intrusive thoughts kept popping up, and I couldn't put my finger on why. We'd sit cuddled together on our leather couch, and I'd shake my head as I thought about different scenarios. I didn't think the danger would be a plane crash, but it could be. Then, I wondered if maybe Heath was going to fall in love with someone else there, and maybe that was the worry. I didn't know how to explain it. I had no real answers to put to my fear and anxiety, but I felt like all I could do, again, was to leave it up to God. I tried my very best to remain positive, and I ignored the deep knowing in my gut that something might go wrong.

The guys headed off to Athens and the islands, and Heath called to check in a couple of times, telling me about some of their adventures. It wasn't until I was parked at the curb at the Spokane airport ten days later to pick him up that I knew something terrible had happened while he was away, and that my premonition *had* meant something. Heath slid into the passenger seat, and as soon as he leaned over to kiss me hello, my eyes immediately went to one of his eyebrows. It was obvious he'd had stitches recently, and he was sporting what looked like the end stage of a huge black eye. I felt sick to my stomach as he somberly explained that he'd been jumped by a bunch of Greeks the very first morning on one of the islands.

When the guys were visiting Greece, the US government was warning tourists to avoid that country because there had been a lot of turbulence due to terrorist attacks and the nearby air war in Yugoslavia. But Heath was half Greek, and I think that made us all feel safer about their journey abroad. No one would attack a Greek American, right?

Wrong. While Jared and John ordered food a few feet away that very first day, Heath asked a local if they could sit at his table. For some reason, a fight broke out between him and several locals, likely fishermen, and he ended up being beaten so severely that Jared had to carry Heath out of the little dockside restaurant to get him out of the dangerous situation before it escalated even further.

It took years for Jared and Heath to tell me the full story. Heath had almost just died only six months earlier.

His poor, concussed head and neck were still healing. They were just trying to provide me some peace, I know, by not sharing all the gritty, shitty details. I knew it had to have been horrific when Heath admitted that he didn't get to leave the hotel room until the last day of the trip because he was so injured. He told me that a priest had performed his stitches in a small church. The man's hands shook the whole time because he'd never sewn a stitch before.

Thank God Heath came back home to me after that trip, even if he was in broken pieces. It just cemented in my mind that we were going to have a long, happy life. How could we not live like that when Heath had survived so much? When we'd already been through so much as a young couple?

Unbelievably, he did not experience any negative side effects after that trip to Greece, and by the fall of that year, we were pregnant with our firstborn and eager to just live a normal life, free of injuries, hospitals, and worry. We even took a babymoon trip with another close couple to Italy a few months before we were due, always making the most of our time together because we knew just how precious it was.

When I was eight and a half months pregnant that summer, the Seattle heat got to be too much for us in our old brick house, and it was suffocating to be so pregnant without air conditioning. After getting the go-ahead from my doctor that the baby wouldn't arrive for at least two more weeks, we hopped on a ferry to a rental on Whidbey Island that we shared with our dear friends Scott and Liz Lisle. They were also expecting their first baby just a few weeks behind us, and they were the couple we traveled to Italy with for our babymoons.

Apparently, our baby had plans of his own, and my water broke at one in the morning. There's nothing like knowing you're going to give birth soon and being stuck on an island without ferry service in the middle of the night! Fortunately for us, there is a road back to Seattle, but it takes a couple of hours to get there. We threw our things in the Pathfinder, grabbed our dog, Louie, and started making our way home. As I sat on a towel, writing down the timing of my contractions and calling our moms so they could make arrangements to fly over for the birth, Heath hauled ass to get us back home and get my hospital bag, which I hadn't finished packing.

When we arrived at the ER, the nurse tried to send us home. She said that my water hadn't been broken that long, my contractions were still too far apart, and we could wait it out at home. We told her we weren't leaving because my contractions were two minutes apart! Finally, after a call to our doctor, we were given the okay to be checked into a room. It was a good thing, too, because just a few hours later, our sweet, blue-eyed Nickolas "Niko" Bruce

McHenry arrived and was the perfect (day-before) Father's Day present!

Our daughter, MaryKate Dyan, was born in early May, less than two years later, and she and Niko became the best of friends. When I was pregnant with her, the news of 9/11 unfolded in front of our eyes as Heath and I watched *The Today Show* cover the tragedy. We were so worried about bringing another child into a world that was hurting so deeply, but we were ecstatic to welcome our beautiful little girl and prayed we would be a happy, healthy family of four. She was the perfect little baby, sleeping through the night almost immediately and smiling, with her head of bouncing brown curls and bright-blue eyes, just like her daddy and brother. We were all smitten.

2004

Heath and I loved living in Seattle and raising our two toddlers there. We had kind and reliable college-aged babysitters—Nicole, Sarah, and Rachel—so we were often able to go out on date nights. Many of our best conversations happened when we were sitting around restaurant tables or driving together in the car. We were always making plans for new adventures, and Heath loved to plan for our future. Our favorite musician, Dave Matthews, lived in our neighborhood, and it was fun to run into him and his family here and there. It was also kind of funny because a few times, the baristas at our local Starbucks mistook Heath for Dave. It gave us both a good giggle every time!

We realized one day, though, that as our children got older, we wanted them to grow up near our families. So, while renting a cute, farmhouse-style home in one of our favorite Seattle neighborhoods, Wallingford, we designed and built a home back in Liberty Lake. Two years later, we moved our little family of four back to the east side of the state and looked forward to raising them how we grew up—in a smaller town surrounded by family.

Almost as soon as we moved to the lake and got settled, so did my best friend Laurie, her husband Jeff, and their young daughter Kate. Having them down the road gave MaryKate a built-in playmate, and I got to see my bestie whenever I wanted. As the months and years passed, our circle of friends grew to be more of a village of couples and their families. If we weren't all at the lake, you could probably find lots of us together on the ski slopes at Schweitzer Mountain.

That first winter living in Liberty Lake, I got to see Heath's passion for snow skiing for myself. I had never been skiing with him and didn't grow up a skier, but I knew that teaching our children to ski was the ultimate dream for him. Before I knew it, we were renting a ski condo in nearby Idaho and taking our two-year-old and four-year-old to the mountains almost every weekend. If you want to test a marriage, even a strong one, try getting two toddlers bundled in ski gear and on skis at the same time. So much work!

I can honestly tell you now that I had absolutely no idea what I had signed up for when I agreed to go along with Heath's ski adventures. By the time Niko was five, he was ski racing with the Schweitzer Alpine Racing Team (SARS), and MaryKate followed shortly after. I had to learn to control my fear of possible accidents and injuries because they loved it almost as much as their dad did. Granted, as toddlers, it took them a while to love it and enjoy getting up for the first bell or skiing in crummy conditions, but they stuck with it. We became permanent fixtures up at Schweitzer Mountain, volunteered for the ski team when the kids raced, traveled with other families to different mountains, and basically built what felt like a ski family to rely on up there. Between Liberty Lake and the mountain, our lives were full of friends and family who loved and supported us.

In August 2005, Heath and I celebrated our seventh wedding anniversary, and in true McHenry style, we threw a huge party for our friends and family. We had a great turnout, complete with an ice luge for shots of booze, live music, dancing, and, of course, ouzo. At one point, I was mingling with some of our neighbors on our back patio when an uninvited guest opened our gate and stepped into our yard. As he walked up the stairs toward me, I could see he was either inebriated or on drugs. I asked nicely whom he was coming to visit. Instead of answering me, he immediately began calling me some nasty names and trying to push past me. The men around me kept trying to get him to leave, but it escalated quickly.

In less than a minute, Heath had heard the scuffle and was right by my side, urging the man to leave before things got worse. The guy would not take no for an answer and kept berating me and others. He reminded me of a wild animal, in a way. I felt so much safer with Heath right next to me. He always, always made me feel safe.

After a few more minutes of this man arguing with my husband and trying to get past us, Heath stepped forward and headbutted him right in the face! I heard the thump. It was so loud! The guy tumbled backward down the stairs and was carried away by several of our friends, but even after all that, he kept trying to come back. Police were finally called to escort him from the neighborhood. He was so high on drugs that they had to taser him to quiet him down.

I share this story because, first, it's kind of romantic how my husband stood up for me. But also, it's a perfect example of how incredibly protective Heath was of me and any of his loved ones. Fighting never scared him. Anyone who messed with him was in trouble.

January 2006

This was one of those times when you realize just how quickly life can change in an instant. It's not like I didn't already know that, especially being married to Heath. But wow, my husband must have been like a cat with nine lives.

Heath, our friend Jim Joy, and Laurie's husband Jeff drove to Canada to go helicopter skiing. Remember how stressed out that idea made me when Dr. Erlich brought it up seven years earlier? Well, being Heath's wife and knowing how much joy skiing gave him, I agreed to this trip, which was the second heli-ski vacation I had agreed to. Getting dropped off by a helicopter onto a big, snowy mountain that an average skier could not access was something Heath and his ski buddies loved.

Because I wasn't there that day, I'm going to let Jeff tell you about the event that could have changed our lives forever but, thankfully, did not:

THE HUSBAND ON LOAN FROM HEAVEN

Six of us were all seated knee to knee in a helicopter on the few-minute flight to the top of the mountain in Nelson, BC. Heath was to my left, and Jim and I were basically bumping kneecaps.

Heath had expressed some concerns about the validity of our pilot in the event that any type of inclement weather should occur (i.e., wind, fog, heavy snow, etc.). Heavy fog did roll in, and Heath had observed that the pilot had circled our intended landing spot at least two times. With his aviation background from college, Heath's eyes were wide open. I believe it was much like a race car driver would pay attention during a New York City cab ride!

On about our third approach, our pilot's angle was off, and we had a tail strike into the snow, ice, and rocks. Evidently, when this happens, pilots are trained to immediately slam the body of the helicopter to the ground. In our case, multiple feet of powder somewhat pillowed our hard landing. Still, it was startling. We were all wondering the same thing: *Are we safe now? Or are we going to slide down the side of this mountain in the helicopter?*

The helicopter blades came to a stop, and we were all instructed to climb out. On a positive note or two, there were no injuries (yet), and we got to ski down. As you could imagine, we chose to switch to cat skiing for the rest of the trip instead of taking another helicopter.

The next day, Jim got caught up in an avalanche and blew out his ACL. Heath ended up driving Jim's car back home to Spokane, and I drove Jim directly to the hospital for treatment.

For those who aren't familiar with it, Cat skiing originated in Canada when someone came up with the fantastic idea of using the robust, tracked vehicles (known as snowcats) that groom downhill ski slopes to transport skiers up the mountain in search of steeper slopes and fresh powder. It's now a very common adventure available on many ski hills.

I share this story with you because it was just one more time Heath could have easily lost his life. Thankfully, this time, he made it out unscathed.

2008–2018

In April 2008, we had our third child, Smith Alexander, and he completed our little McHenry party of five. We had thought we would stop at two kiddos years earlier. However, as I neared forty, I realized, and so did Heath, that we wanted to have another baby. Niko and MaryKate had been asking for a sibling, so we told them to pray for one. I remember sitting at an outdoor table at Tito's Italian Restaurant in Coeur d'Alene with the kids as Heath told them their prayers worked! It was such a sweet moment for the four of us. They were ecstatic, and so were we.

This is one of those times when I want to tell you that you'll never regret having another child, but you might regret that you didn't. Smith came out with his own unique personality, somewhat of an old soul, from the minute he was born. He never (and by never, I mean only once) slept in his crib and would not eat baby food in any form. But he was the perfect little brother and son for us.

When he was two, Smith was already a little pro on skis and making turns on the snow with us on all the mountains we traveled to for Niko's and MaryKate's ski races. In November 2010, I stayed back at home with him while Heath drove the other kids to Panorama Mountain, Canada, for training. What happened on that mountain that week was one more glaring time my husband survived what could have been an otherwise fatal accident.

One morning, he wanted to buy Smith a t-shirt he had seen in a window at the ski shop, but he headed to the nearby café to grab his Americano first. He got to the steps right in front of the café and stopped, overwhelmed with the feeling that he was supposed to go buy the t-shirt first. He turned and walked over to the ski shop, bought the shirt, and was away from the stairs by the coffee shop for no more than three or four minutes at the most. When he walked back toward the café, he immediately saw why he had felt compelled to *not* go in there first.

A ski patroller driving his snowmobile had lost control, and the snowmobile had barreled straight down the mountain, over those stairs, and right into the front of the café—exactly where Heath would have been standing to order his Americano. The snowmobile was still running, slowed down only by its collision with the front door and cash register stand. Miraculously, no one was hurt.

After gathering his thoughts and realizing what an incredibly close call that was, Heath stood by those broken steps and felt immediately, and intuitively, that it was his beloved grandmother, YiaYia Pauline, who had saved him. The phenomenal truth was that she had just passed away only five days earlier, back in Spokane.

Of course, over the years, there were other instances of my husband having near misses and severe concussions that could have easily caused permanent damage, or even death. Every time, he managed to end up being stronger than ever—like a boxer who gets knocked down but always wins. *Unstoppable* is the word that comes to mind. He never ceased to amaze me or anyone who knew him.

Over the next decade, we worked hard together to raise our children the best way we knew how, and we made a great team. One of the reasons we got along so well was that we always communicated, even when we knew it might be a tough conversation.

Heath loved to coach—along with his close dad friends—all three of our kids and many of their young friends in t-ball, baseball, and football. He was very supportive of them being in sports, and also very passionate about it. Like many sports parents, he could sometimes go a little overboard with that passion and push the kids beyond what they felt good with, causing them to *not* want to participate at times. Thankfully, over the years, I learned to use my own voice as their mom to help keep the peace, and it helped us become stronger as parents and a couple. We didn't just let the stress simmer. We talked it out. Heath was a great listener. Of course, we didn't always end up agreeing on everything, but we always felt heard by each other. I'm so grateful to have had a husband who listened.

One of my favorite things about our relationship is that we both loved to travel, and that didn't change when we had our children. We taught them to love adventure, too. We traveled with them from a very young age to faraway countries, like Greece, Italy, and France. Many of our spring breaks were spent in Hawaii, and we always found a way to visit the beach in Oregon or on the California coast in the summer. We also made an annual trip to Mt. Hood, Oregon, each July for a summer ski camp that became one of our favorites. Many of the other ski families from Schweitzer would join us, so the kids had built-in friends, and we could have lots of fun adult time, too. Everyone looked forward to that adventure. Even today, as I write this in 2024, our youngest, Smith, is heading to Mt. Hood. Some traditions are too good to end! We even spent years of Thanksgivings in Canada with our SARS ski family so all the kids could train on man-made snow. Dozens of us would share a huge potluck dinner with multiple turkeys and pies, and we'd cheer on the kids during their annual Turkey Cup race at the end of the week.

Whether we were traveling, skiing, boating, watching the kids' sports, hiking on our property behind our house, taking an adventure, or just hanging out at home, our McHenry party of five was a solid unit, and I couldn't have asked for a better, more loyal man to raise our children with.

Many times over the years, we encountered scary health problems with our children (concussions, Lyme disease, broken bones, lymphangioma surgery, etc.). And just as I did when Heath was lying on that floor in the firehouse in Lake Forest Park back in 1999, I used my voice to advocate for them. If I can share one vital lesson that I have learned as a mother (and wife), it's that you have to follow your gut instinct, no matter what any medical professional says. You have to speak up, no matter how uncomfortable it might be, if you're going to get the answers you need. Let Mama Bear out if you have to. These are your precious loved ones—the little pieces of your heart who walk around outside your body. Learn to advocate for them and for yourself. You'll only grow stronger in the process. I can assure you of that!

One glaring example of advocating for my family and using my voice as a mom was when our daughter was twelve. She became sick with a mystery illness, and it took over a year to be diagnosed correctly. Those twelve months we spent taking her to doctors, hospitals, and clinics took a toll on all of us because no one would believe her symptoms. She missed all of eighth grade and had to watch on Instagram and Snapchat as her friends went about their lives. It was such a traumatic time for our family, and it was often made worse because of the doctors who didn't listen to us. She and I both ended up with PTSD (post-traumatic stress disorder). When she was finally healing and on her road to recovery at the beginning of ninth grade, I found a way to take care of myself and give back to other women at the same time. I created a national conference for moms in order to inspire, celebrate, and encourage them. Helping others who need that kind of support has been a life raft for me over the years. I also started hosting a podcast, *Mama's Gotta Bloom*, to go along with the conferences.

Having Heath and our children support and cheer me on while I took on these passion projects was just what my heart needed to heal.

2020

By the spring of 2020, our family of five was together constantly, stuck at home mostly, thanks to a damn pandemic. I didn't realize at the time how meaningful those long, drawn-out months were until life finally started returning to somewhat normal a year later. I bet some of you can relate to that. Seriously. We were wiping off our mail and groceries with bleach wipes and weren't allowed to go anywhere.

Heath, the kids, and I, along with Heath's mom (affectionately known as YiaYia)—who lives in the house next door to us—ate dinner together often and just enjoyed our downtime. Heath built a home gym so he could continue his daily workouts, and the kids loved to join him. He was so proud of that gym, and working out was something he'd committed to as a teen. We couldn't go out to eat or shop or do many basic things that we were used to, but he made the best out of his time at home by building the gym. He always made the best out of any situation. We were alike in that way, and it was one of my favorite things about us—we could both find a silver lining in the middle of some of the worst times.

The cloud of pandemic darkness that hovered over the entire world slowly started to lift by late 2020. Our older kids had headed off to college earlier in the fall with face masks and mandatory COVID tests, and Smith was trying to focus on online school. Heath was the only one in our family who ended up choosing to get the vaccine. He researched for months prior to making his decision and felt it was the right thing to do for himself. I disagreed with his choice but knew it was up to him. We let Niko and MaryKate make their own choices when it came to getting the COVID vaccination, so when they both decided against it, we sent in formal requests to their universities, thereby requiring the mandatory weekly testing.

Right after we dropped MaryKate off at school that September, she and Heath both ended up sick with COVID. She had to quarantine with friends in Seattle while Heath switched places with his mom, quarantining at her house next door and having her stay at ours. He and I hated those two weeks of not being able to be together, touch, or just sleep in the same bed. We were both so excited to finally make out when his fourteen days were up that we felt like newlyweds. It was so fun and gave us renewed energy. Again, we found the silver lining. We knew we were each other's soulmate, and that fourteen-day stretch somehow sweetened our relationship even more.

Heath's career as a financial advisor continued to go well, and his practice was growing, even amidst all the unrest in our world. I was ready to start up my podcast and in-person events again as soon as I could, as I was missing the connections with other women that my job provided me. Life felt pretty good!

On New Year's Eve at the mountain, we gathered with several of our very close friends—the Hadleys and the Moores—to toast a new year of adventures. Everyone had been cooped up for so long that we decided to plan a couples-only trip to New Orleans that spring. We couldn't wait to get out of town! My main purpose for that trip, besides enjoying my husband and our friends, was to do research for a book I had started writing during the pandemic. It was mainly about vampires and immortals, and I said to Heath, "What better place to research than NOLA—home of the Vampire Café and cemetery tours?"

Always supportive of me and my crazy ideas (and trust me, Scooby had some off-the-wall ones too), he immediately loved the idea, and our vacation was set.

March 4–7, 2021

That group getaway was one of the best vacations we ever took as a couple, and to share it with dear friends was the icing on the cake. Everything just aligned all weekend, and the six of us were in perfect sync. The guys tried deep-fried crocodile, we all went on a ghost and cemetery tour and visited the Vampire Café, and we girls stopped by the local voodoo shop for creepy photos in a coffin set up as a photo prop. Heath would not set foot near that place—he would not even walk on the same block—because it made him so uncomfortable.

He never did like anything to do with death, psychics, tarot cards, or anything related to the spirit world. Even certain songs spooked him. He would hear the song "If I Die Young," by The Band Perry, and immediately change the station every single time. I chalked it up to his having almost died that January day back in 1999 and knowing how quickly life can change. We respected each other's opinions about it for the most part, although I knew his dislike for things like tarot and psychic readings meant those were things he wanted us both to avoid. His mom had seen several psychic mediums over the years, and I found her stories fascinating. Heath wanted nothing to do with it. I was curious about it myself, but not enough to cause disruptions in my relationship with my husband. Heath was extremely supportive of my book about supernatural beings, and that was enough for me. Being in New Orleans and learning about those things with him was such a blessing. I knew I would be able to bounce ideas off him once we were back home and I was writing again. I couldn't wait to finish my book, and he was so proud of what I was accomplishing.

One of my favorite memories of that trip was waiting for our breakfast outside on Royal Street and listening to the street musicians. It was a sunny Saturday, and a trio of ladies stopped their shopping and started dancing in the middle of the road, bringing huge smiles to everyone standing around. I was happily surprised when one of the musicians started to play Louis Armstrong's "What a Wonderful World," which was our wedding song. I look back now and feel like we were meant to hear that song that particular day.

Another favorite part of our NOLA adventure was cruising the Lafayette swamp on an airboat, looking for alligators, and being able to hold a baby one. My checklist for New Orleans was complete!

One thing that stands out now is that while I was packing in our hotel room to leave on our last day, Heath decided to stop by the Hadleys' room and sit for a while to visit. We had just spent the past four days together, but he told me he wanted to say hi to them one more time before we left for the airport. Although we were all heading back to Spokane, we were going home on different flights. Kim and Travis have told me that they will always be grateful for Heath's last-minute decision to do that. At the time, they did not know that would be the last time they would see him.

When we arrived home that Sunday evening, we told our kids how much fun we had and described all the adventures we'd shared with Jason, Sharelynn, Trav, and Kim. Heath and I lay in bed late that night giggling about all the things we'd seen and done. It had been such a great weekend!

The next day, I was scheduled to have a biopsy on my right breast. We had both been stressed about the upcoming appointment all weekend in New Orleans, joking with our friends that we needed to pray for my boob. It had already been a month of worry, so I had tried to clear it from my mind while we were on our vacation. Heath had planned to go with me to my appointment but realized that morning that he had double-booked himself with his second COVID vaccination. I told him I'd be fine and to go ahead. He always knew how to make me feel supported and invincible, and I knew I could handle my appointment on my own. We treated our kids the same way—like they could do anything they set their mind to. I walked into that appointment strong and ready for whatever might be coming. I was scared, of course, but I always felt better and more confident with my husband in my corner.

After spending more than an hour with me that Monday afternoon, the surgeon admitted that, although she had seen all the previous scans, she felt she didn't have a good enough reason to perform a biopsy. She shook her head in disbelief but seemed certain of her diagnosis. I was immediately relieved and at peace with her decision. She sent me on my way, and I texted Heath as soon as I was in my car to tell him the unexpected good news. He texted back right away and said he was so glad and that he loved me.

It felt like a brand-new beginning. No more breast cancer worries. Heath and the kids were mostly healthy. And we were finally free to take off the pandemic masks and live again.

It was a much-needed fresh start.

March 12, 2021

Just four days later, on a beautiful March afternoon with the sun peeking out from behind the cold, clear blue sky, I received a phone call that would change my world forever.

As I stepped out of the shower dripping wet and pulled a towel around me to grab my ringing cell phone, I noticed it was a friend's number calling. I immediately answered because I knew this particular friend, Joe Hamilton, was skiing with my husband that afternoon.

Joe calmly explained that everything was okay as soon as I answered. He said Heath had been in an accident on the hill and that ski patrol had some questions for me. Heath hadn't been able to respond much to them, and they weren't sure what his injuries might be.

Thinking quickly, I asked Joe to put me on FaceTime so I could see my husband. Looking through my cell phone to see him lying still in his ski gear on the crisp white snow made me feel a little better because there were no signs of injury or blood that I could see. His eyes were open, looking toward the sky, and he didn't seem to be in pain. But his breathing sounded shaky. Almost gurgly. The ski patroller leaned in and asked me about Heath's accident in 1999, wondering if this incident could have something to do with that.

All of a sudden, this became a scenario I did not want to be a part of. His taking me back to that first accident, when Heath almost died, did not feel good. I began to panic a little but kept my calm as I stood there in our bathroom— towel wrapped around myself and my wet hair dripping down my back—and answered the man's question. I felt confident in assuring him that the two were likely not related. Heath's neck injury had healed with no further complications over twenty years earlier.

Joe filled me in as fast as he could, explaining that he, Heath, and some of Joe's family had just finished having lunch at Sky House at the top of the hill. After strapping on their skis, Heath skied ahead a bit, looking back once in a while and cheering on James, Joe's five-year-old grandson, who had just been challenged by the group to attempt to ski backward.

The next thing Joe knew, Heath was straddling a snow-covered tree with one arm and one ski on either side of it and his torso right up against it. Joe said his first reaction was to laugh and ask Heath why he was hugging the tree. Heath replied that he had run into it and acted as if he didn't quite understand how it happened either. James saw Heath and apologized for making him run into the tree. Heath, "chivalrous as ever," said Joe, assured James that it was not his fault.

Although Joe was chuckling at the very strange sight of Heath hugging the tree, he told me he could tell Heath was confused a little, so he skied over to him. After unwrapping himself from the tree, Heath skied maybe five yards, then told Joe he felt strange and needed to sit down for a minute. Within five or ten seconds of sitting down, he began having labored breathing and was lying down, mostly unresponsive. Ski patrol was dispatched to help as soon as it was clear Heath was experiencing an emergency.

I listened to Joe's words, trying to think of what could have happened to cause this accident as I stared at my husband through the screen. My heart jumped when I watched Heath's bright-blue eyes track up to the left as he recognized my voice. I spoke to him in his left ear (thank God for FaceTime) and told him he was going to be fine. I said we'd been through this before and would get through it now. I snapped a quick screenshot of him and told him how much I loved him. He didn't reply, and Joe took the phone back, assuring me his daughter, Sydney, had just demanded that a helicopter be deployed because she could sense the urgency of the situation.

Shortly after, a Life Flight landed on the top of the mountain to transport Heath to the nearest hospital. The in-flight nurse used Joe's phone to talk with me, and she confirmed that she would call me from the air so I would know which hospital to drive to. Heath's mountainside rescue was underway, and all I could do was pray for his safety.

As I hurriedly got dressed and made a quick call to a friend to ensure our youngest son was taken care of, I was trying to be optimistic that this accident was not going to turn into a big ordeal. The medical professionals were on top of it, so I knew he was in good hands. Besides, my husband had already almost died more than once. There was no way God would do that to us now. I was sure of it.

That hopeful but naive feeling I was holding on to so hard started to go sideways when more calls began coming in from Laurie and from Joe's wife Sarah. Soon, it was apparent that maybe I was not taking this accident seriously enough. If I had any question in my mind about whether or not to start worrying, I got my answer when the nurse did not call me from the Life Flight.

Overwhelmed and now frantic about what I should do next, I started by calling the two closest hospitals. Either one would be about a twenty-minute drive away. One was in Idaho and the other in Washington. The operator at Spokane's Sacred Heart Medical Center didn't have any helicopters scheduled to land, so I dialed Kootenai Health in Idaho next. The operator there said an ambulance was coming from Schweitzer, but I knew in my heart that it had to be Heath and that it was actually a helicopter.

Hoping I was doing the right thing, I called Heath's mom's best friend, Pat, and warned her that she needed to come and be with MaryLou as soon as possible, due to what seemed like the rising severity of the situation.

Not wanting to alarm MaryLou any more than necessary, I jumped in my car and drove next door to her house. I explained as calmly as I could that there had been an accident and that I was on my way to (what I hoped was) the correct hospital. I told her that Pat was on her way to be with her. Then I kissed the top of MaryLou's head and told her I loved her and would call as soon as I knew anything.

As I headed down Liberty Drive—my heart pumping out of my chest and overwhelming worry clouding my thoughts—I saw Laurie and our friend Kim waiting in front of Laurie's house, eagerly ready to jump in my car with me. But I knew I couldn't stop. I knew time was ticking for me to get to my husband. Something felt off. I knew I needed to see him as soon as I could. I drove right past them, shaking my head, convinced that if I got to the hospital in time, Heath would be okay.

The Life Flight nurse finally called as I pulled onto the freeway entrance toward Idaho. I was shaking as she spoke and was frustrated that she hadn't called earlier. That came through in my tone. She responded that she hadn't been able to call. She sounded just as stressed as I was, explaining quickly that Heath had stopped breathing on the flight and the whole team had been working hard to bring him back.

As I heard that less-than-hopeful news, a rush of adrenaline kicked in faster than I'd ever felt before. My body began visibly trembling as she confirmed that I was heading to the correct hospital.

Before hanging up, she warned me that I needed to hurry.

"You Need to Hurry"

That one sentence—"You need to hurry"—sent me over the edge. I knew it was bad. I couldn't deny it, no matter how badly I wanted to.

Huge, salty, wet tears began to roll down my cheeks as I hung up and drove east on I-90, doing my best to see through the curtain of sobs. The sheer dread of what was unfolding that afternoon began to sink in. I kept looking out my left window, hoping someone driving by, even a passenger, would notice me in my anguished state and pull over to drive me. I still don't know how I managed to make it to the hospital in one piece.

I tried to control my tears and shaking body as I parked close to the ER entrance. My legs were so wobbly that they felt like Jell-O, as if they would give way if I stood up from my driver's seat. I looked around to see if anyone could help me and noticed a woman to my left. She looked to be around my age, and I noticed her grabbing a lunch bag from the passenger side of her car. I guessed she worked there, and I called out to her from my open door, begging her to help me walk with me because I knew I couldn't do it by myself. I told her I thought my husband was dying and begged her to just get me inside. I'm so grateful she was there that day, right when I needed her. She immediately took my arm and walked with me through the front doors of the ER, murmuring kind words I don't remember. Whoever she is, I hope she knows that she was an angel sent to me that day.

As soon as we entered, the young girl at the front desk looked overwhelmed at the sight of me. I tried to calmly ask where my husband was, but I was not calm. My teeth were chattering incessantly, and my whole body felt numb as I tried to hold back tears long enough to ask her if my husband was there or if he had died.

I felt like I was in the twilight zone, as if I'd stepped into another dimension that wasn't real. Uncontrollable waves of terror took over my whole being as I tried to stand still. Nothing was making sense. It was all a blur. Someone brought me back to Heath's room, and they said I could stand right outside it.

I was immediately grateful to see my precious husband—my Scooby—lying unconscious in that room, and I watched with a heavy, heavy heart as a huge team of medical personnel in the lightest of yellow scrubs worked intensely to revive him. What I saw sucked the air right out of me. I rocked myself back and forth like one rocks a baby. I needed to soothe myself, and it helped. I felt a little more in control of my emotions. I began to pray to God as hard as I could outside that hospital room, just like I had twenty-two years earlier in Seattle.

Only a few minutes went by, but it seemed like years. Then I felt a light tap on my shoulder. I looked back to my left and saw a kind-eyed gentleman in a sweater vest standing behind me, his face full of concern. I don't remember everything he said, but I felt his calming presence. He told me that if I needed anything, he was there for me. Not wanting to take my eyes off Heath for more than a second, I glanced back quickly and replied to him in no uncertain terms, "Just don't call the chaplain," before I set my gaze back on my husband.

"I am the chaplain," he replied softly.

My heart sank. Not knowing what else to do and feeling utterly alone and scared, I told him he could stay. He asked if I wanted to be with Heath inside the room while the team worked on him, and I was dumbfounded. Of course I did.

I nodded, and he urged me to move into the room, gently leading me in by the arm and telling me to try to step anywhere on the floor where there wasn't blood.

I am not exaggerating when I say the entire room looked like a murder scene from *Dexter* (one of Heath's and my favorite shows) because the linoleum was covered in puddles of bright-red liquid. A very large incision had been made on Heath's left side during the flight. I watched as the bag of donated blood pumping through the IV to Heath's veins on the right side of his body just splashed out from that open left side and onto the previously light-colored hospital floor.

I quietly observed all the people who were trying to save my husband's life that day as I walked somberly into the room and stationed myself to the left of his head. I began to rub his temples, which he always loved, and whispered to him, trying to stay out of the way. "Scooby, I love you," I said. Everything is going to be fine. We've done this before. It's okay. You'll be okay."

"Where is his wedding ring?" I asked with annoyance as soon as I realized his left ring finger was bare. "He has never taken it off once. Please, put it back on him now!"

"I'm sorry. That's just our usual protocol!" one of the nurses replied as she retrieved the ring.

Before she put it back on his finger, I asked her to let me see it up close. I had had the inside engraved with our initials for our wedding, but I had not seen it since the day we got married. Heath never, and I mean never, took off his ring. The engraving—8/22/98 KELSY AND HEATH— jumped out at me, and I was so relieved to see it. It just reminded me that no matter what—even through this awful, awful nightmare we were living at the moment—we would always be together.

Soon after, the ring was back in its rightful spot. So much was going wrong that day. The last thing I wanted or needed was to see one more piece of Heath not as it should be.

The ER doctor, a blonde woman with her hair pulled back in a ponytail, looked like she could be one of my Liberty Lake friends. It was comforting, in a way. She introduced herself as Dr. Jackson and explained that she was holding Heath's blood vessels inside his chest together with her thumb and finger to stop the bleeding. I could hear the stress in her voice. Listening to her words made me nauseous, further adding to my growing fear that the likelihood of him not surviving this accident was becoming all too real.

It didn't help ease my rising panic that there was a huge metal device sticking right out of the top of his chest. To me, it looked like a big silver sprinkler part that someone would use to water their crops, just like the ones I used to help my grandpa with on his farm. I later learned that this device is used to open the chest cavity to give easier access during trauma care. But to me, it looked like there was no way someone could survive even that.

I kept looking at the left side of Heath's body, the one the doctor was working on, where the blood continued to splash right out of his torso and onto the floor. I couldn't understand why someone hadn't already stitched part of the incision back together so more of the blood would stay inside his body. My mind was spinning with questions.

Wouldn't that help? Couldn't that maybe save him? These are questions I'll never know the answers to. I didn't ask them out loud. The team was already so busy trying to get his heart to restart that I didn't want to interrupt the lifesaving process they were so engrossed in.

Nothing happening in the scene in front of me made any sense. All I could see and smell was blood, and all I could feel was crippling fear. I was terrified, more scared than I've been in my entire life. I prayed and prayed. And I tried to trick myself into believing that everything was going to go just like I wanted and needed it to. Heath was a freaking badass, and he could survive anything. He already had, several times. He would start breathing again, his eyes would flutter open like they had back in 1999 in that Seattle emergency room, and he would be fine.

But, as the minutes passed, I began to realize I was in absolute denial. Each time the defibrillator didn't restart his heart, I felt more and more profound dread. I tried to keep myself preoccupied by looking at Heath's face as much as possible because it was just his beautiful, flawless face. There were no cuts, bruises, or blood on it that I could see. A blue-and-white breathing tube had been placed between his teeth, but other than that, his handsome Greek profile looked the same as always.

The kind, young nurse standing on Heath's right continually checked the pulse in his neck for any sign of movement. Once in a while, she'd seem hopeful, but then she would shake her head. I could tell she wanted so badly to be able to say she felt something moving in there.

One person stood in light-yellow scrubs on a chair at the foot of Heath's gurney and seemed to be the one monitoring all the timing. I watched the big group work together as a team, and it was obvious they wanted to bring my husband back for me.

Unfortunately, God had other plans for us that afternoon.

On March 12, 2021, at 5:18 p.m., Heath went home to Heaven.

How do I know?

Because as the days after he passed went by, it became very apparent to me that he had been on loan to me from God. For twenty-two years, God had given me Heath so we could build our lives together, have our three beautiful children, and continue our love story.

My faith became stronger over the months after he died. I knew God had listened to my prayers that first traumatic January day back in 1999. He had heard me. He let me, our children, MaryLou, and all our family and friends have our wonderful Heath for all those years so we could love him and learn from him.

For that, I'm eternally grateful.

After

How do you tell your three precious children that their adored father—their best friend and hero—has just died?

I call this the after part of my journey because life as you know it stops after someone who is your whole life dies. You will never be the same as you were before they passed away. You will be so different that you might not even recognize yourself sometimes. I knew that as soon as I broke the awful, unimaginable news to our children, none of us would ever be the same. We would never be the same happy, energetic, and peaceful family of five we were when Heath was here. I had no idea what to expect, let alone what life would look like for us as a family of four.

So, this is *my* after. Welcome to what it's like to lose your person and yourself in a matter of minutes.

March 12, 2021, 5:30 P.M.

Once I had been escorted from the ER, where Heath's body still lay, to a small, private area where a few of us gathered (Laurie, Kim, YiaYia, Pat, Chaplain Paul, and me), the only word I could even manage to get out of my mouth was "Fuck."

I sat down, clumps of tissue in my hands, and shook with fear as I tried to take it all in. My mind was so overwhelmed that I couldn't think straight. The acute shock of what had just happened was setting in. Numbness began to settle in my veins as I kept repeating the f-word, not caring how I sounded. There is no rule book for just losing your husband, so I let myself feel whatever came to me.

I immediately knew I needed to call our oldest child, Niko, first because he was a thousand miles away at college in San Diego. He would have to catch the next flight out to make it back home that night, and it was essential that we all be together. Our family was (and is) so close. We have always been there for each other, no matter what. This time would be no different. We would embrace, love, and support each other as a family, but this time would not feel the same. It would be the beginning of the end of days as the family we knew. Our worlds would shift, and we would have to learn to survive and thrive as a family of four. Without our hero. Without our rock.

I will never—and I mean *never*—forget the dismay and deep, deep heartache I felt having to FaceTime my twenty-year-old son. As soon as Niko answered in his usual upbeat tone, I saw that he was driving and told him to pull over right away. He heard the anguish in my voice, and his face filled with despair.

"You're worrying me, Mom."

"Just please pull over, honey. But be safe."

With two of his best college friends in the car listening, I had to deliver the horrific news. Niko opened his door and fell to his knees. Looking to the sky and crying in disbelief, he yelled, "No! Why, God? Please, why God?"

That's an image I will never forget, the breaking of my own child's heart.

As Niko spoke to me through his tears, one serendipitous thing stood out. He pointed to the t-shirt he was wearing, yelling, "Mom! Mom! My shirt!"

I gasped as I read the words printed on his shirt.

LOOK DEATH IN THE EYE

Niko was wearing a shirt he had bought just a couple of weeks prior. At the time, little did he know that it would become a motto he would choose to live by for the rest of his life.

Although I wished I could have talked to him for longer, time was of the essence. We told each other, "I love you," several times, and I quickly explained that Laurie's husband, Uncle Jeff, would be arranging Niko's flight back to Spokane. Within an hour, he was somehow at the airport, packed, and ready to come home. That two-and-a-half-hour flight was surely the longest of his young life, but he did share later that he felt comforted because he saw his dad and his Bapa Bruce (Heath's late father) outside his passenger window that evening, flying alongside the airplane.

As if telling Niko over the phone wasn't hard enough for this mama heart, I next had to FaceTime our daughter, MaryKate. She was a freshman at the University of Washington in Seattle. As soon as she picked up the phone, I could see she was in great spirits and surrounded by a handful of her Gamma Phi sorority sisters. By this time, I was barely in survival mode, but I gently explained what had happened to her dad, who also happened to be her best friend and workout partner.

MaryKate was always Heath's little *koukla*, his endearing term for her that comes from the Greek word meaning "doll or little doll." The shock and sadness of my words immediately registered on her radiant face, and I watched as the small group (who I later learned were in the middle of taking an online final) absorbed what I had just said. Within minutes, we had made a plan to have a good friend fly home with her so she wouldn't have to travel alone.

I'm forever grateful that MaryKate and Niko landed at the airport shortly after each other and were able to come back home together that night. I'm also grateful for our friends who picked them up and loved on them during such a traumatic time. It really does take a village.

With Niko and MaryKate both on the way home, I was slightly relieved but also filled with dread that I had another grueling call to make. Trying to stifle the huge tears that wanted to stream down my cheeks, I took a few deep breaths, muttered some more f-bombs to myself, and then patted my face dry with a tissue.

My next call would be to our youngest, Smith. I was too afraid to tell him about Heath's accident over FaceTime, so I called to tell him that I'd be home soon. I knew it would be best to deliver the news to him in person. He had been waiting all afternoon for me with his good friend and neighbor, Griffin, and he was expecting to drive up to

Schweitzer with me to meet Heath for the weekend. The problem was, Smith was only twelve, just a preteen, but he is wicked smart and somewhat intuitive. He had already seen from our locations on our cell phones that Heath and I were both at a hospital twenty minutes away in Idaho. He called me out on it, demanding to know why we were there. I was trembling so badly that my teeth were chattering. My heart plummeted. I didn't want to tell him like this.

The other complication is that Smith is like his dad—persistent in a good way and won't take no for an answer if he doesn't have to. I tentatively looked over at Chaplain Paul, my worried, tear-filled eyes looking for guidance. He nodded—and so did everyone else in the small hospital waiting room as I looked around—gently urging me to be honest with Smith before the situation could get any worse.

Smith and Griffin were watching me intently through Smith's cell phone, both of them perched at our kitchen counter like it was any other normal afternoon. I looked directly at Griffin and spoke to him first. I needed him to know how important and life-changing this conversation was going to be for Smith, and I wanted to make sure he could be there for my child if needed, even though he was a child himself.

"Griff," I said gently, "I need you to be the best friend you can possibly be right now, okay?"

He nodded with his quiet demeanor. Knowing there was no way around it now, I took my eyes off Griffin and looked over at my precious boy, knowing I was about to break another heart, and I delivered the awful news to Smith.

Fortunately, I had called Griffin's mom, Jacquelin, on my way to the hospital to let her know Heath had been in a bad accident. I asked her to head to our home so the boys wouldn't be alone until I could get back there. At the time, I had no idea that the afternoon would take such a horrendous turn, and that I'd have to tell Smith before she could get there. I'm grateful she was able to get to our house to be there for him (and her own son as he processed what just happened to his friend's dad) shortly after I hung up with Smith. Again, it takes a village, and I'm so grateful for ours.

I will tell you that my heart aches like a freshly opened wound every single time I think about those three FaceTime calls. It also aches for Griffin and the other young friends who were with my children that fateful day when I had to tell them that their strong, confident, handsome Greek god of a dad had died.

Leaving Behind Love

After arranging to bring our children back to the hospital the next morning to say goodbye to their father, I thanked Chaplain Paul and left MaryLou and her friend to say their own goodbyes. I knew her heart was ripping out of her chest, and I couldn't bear to watch.

Carrying a small plastic bag with Heath's Apple Watch and iPhone inside, I walked silently with Laurie down the long hospital corridor, leaving behind my person of almost twenty-six years. The love of my life.

I felt like I was being suffocated. It was so hard to breathe. Once we were situated in my car, Laurie began driving us back toward home, and my mind started racing with thoughts of who needed to know immediately about Heath. I knew that the next call needed to be to Jared, Heath's best friend since middle school and one of the last people to be with him before his accident. They had skied together most of that bluebird day, and then Heath had continued to make a few more runs with the Hamiltons. There was no way I could FaceTime this grown man to break the horrible, unexpected news. Another heart was about to be broken, and I knew I wouldn't be able to handle watching live, for the fourth time, as I delivered the bad news.

I dialed Jared's number on my cell phone and burst into tears. Using the nickname Heath had given Jared years earlier, I said, "Smack. He died."

"No, he didn't!" he wailed.

"Yes, he did."

I can still hear "No, he didn't" over and over again when I think about this call, as he repeated it until the dark truth finally sank in. He thought, like I always had, that his best friend was invincible. Instead, Heath would remain forever forty-nine.

I thank God all the time for *my* best friend Laurie and her unwavering love for my family and me. She has kept me grounded since we were twelve years old, and that fateful day was no different. Heath was like a brother to her, so her pain was just as raw.

IN HER WORDS:

March 12 was a beautiful blue-sky, early-spring day. Our husbands were both at Schweitzer, so you and I went on a late-afternoon walk. Your plan was to then get ready and drive to the mountain to meet up with Heath to go out to dinner with friends. You had no idea what life-changing events were about to unfold. I went inside and set my phone down. Then I walked back outside, loaded some Goodwill bags into my car, and stopped to talk with a neighbor. By the time I went back inside, I had missed several calls from you, Sarah Hamilton, and Kim Goldfeldt. Sarah said it was bad and that we needed to get you to the hospital now. I tried calling you, but there was no answer. In the meantime, Kim drove over to find me so I could drive you, but as we walked outside, you passed us. We immediately got in her car and headed toward Idaho, hoping that was the right direction.

I had another conversation during the car ride with Sarah, who said we should probably get Niko and MaryKate home. I called Jeff and explained that Heath had been in an accident and that we were rushing to Kootenai, where we thought the helicopter would be landing, to learn more. I asked him if he could start looking at flights for the kids, just in case. All along, I was thinking that this sounded like a bad accident, but it was Heath . . . so everything would be okay.

Unsure that we were even in the right place, Kim and I pulled into the hospital parking lot as I continued to try to reach you. I didn't want to call the kids and alarm them until I knew what was happening. I knew they would want details. I had none.

A few agonizing minutes passed . . . and then you called me.

"He died. Heath died. Can you come here?" you asked.

"I'm here," I said. "I'm in the parking lot."

You let me know that the chaplain would meet me at the hospital entrance. Kim asked if she should come or not, and we agreed she should.

I called Jeff and said, "We need the flights . . . Heath didn't make it, but the kids don't know yet."

The next few hours are forever etched in my mind. MaryLou walking in, completely pale and shocked. You FaceTiming Niko, then MaryKate, and seeing their reactions. Then the hard decision to tell Smith because he had your location and you could tell from his voice that he knew something was wrong. You looked at the chaplain, and he nodded, agreeing that you should proceed.

After some time, it was just us in the sitting room. You were handed a small bag of Heath's belongings—I think his watch and phone. You handed me your keys, and we walked down a long, dark hallway and out of the hospital to your car without Heath.

Just a Ziplock bag.

Never could I have imagined that we'd be taking that evening walk.

The ride home was a bit of a blur as you tried to think of all of the critical people you should contact before news traveled. I believe the first was Jared, then your sister, Merytt. You asked her to tell your mom. Then you called Glenn, who would likely start the chain of texts to the neighborhood friends. We arrived at your house. Smith was shaking and crying. We sat with him on the couch, wrapped in a blanket. You assured him it was going to be okay. He was so worried and had many questions.

"Will we have to move?"

"How will we get money?"

"Are you gonna marry someone else?"

"Why?"

Friends and neighbors started coming over . . . I vaguely remember who all was there.

We all sat around in shock, crying and trying to make sense of it. Soon, it was time to pick up the kids from the airport. Kate offered to come with me. It was unimaginable how terrible that flight had to be for both Niko and MaryKate.

MaryKate was the first to land. She was pale but tried to cheerfully say goodbye to the friend who'd flown with her for support. We hugged and sat in silence for a bit, waiting for Niko to arrive.

MaryKate got up and asked the TSA agent if she could meet her brother at his gate. But of course this was against policy, even under the circumstances. The agent was kind and gave MK a hug. It was clear she wanted a moment with Niko alone. When he arrived, they hugged immediately—a long, grieving hug.

I'm pretty sure the TSA agent was crying, too. After their moment alone, we all hugged and walked to the car.

When we got to your house, neither Niko nor MaryKate was ready to face everyone who had gathered, so we decided I'd go in, get you and Smith, and bring you both outside for a moment alone, as family.

The beginning of an unexpected journey as a family of four, minus Heath.

Friday Night

Those first few hours at home are really hazy in my mind, but I remember that friends and family started trickling in, hugging us in disbelief, and crying as they arrived. Several people brought food to snack on, and as the house filled with our loved ones, I would step aside once in a while to make another heart-wrenching call to the next person in line I could think of.

Early in the evening, my glass of pinot grigio glued to my hand, I phoned Heath's assistant, Candice. I had never needed to call her on a personal level before. I'd mainly chatted with her when she was at work with Heath. She was obviously surprised to hear from me on a Friday night and completely blindsided when I told her what had happened. Heath and Candice had been working side by side for twenty-two years. She'd joined his financial practice soon after his first brush with death in April 1999.

Candice was always his wingman at work. That didn't change when Heath died. She would end up being my lifeline at their company for months after that call, as I leaned on her to help me get through our family financials and steer me through the logistics of closing his financial practice.

As the evening wore on, everyone took turns sharing Heath stories, and it was a time of deep connection for all of us there. I would go from lying on the living room floor, sobbing with several others because the couches and chairs were full of grievers, to getting up and walking around in a daze.

The beautiful home we had built together twelve years earlier was filled to the brim that night with loved ones, and it continued to be that way for months after. It became a cozy place to gather and grieve, and the kids and I never knew who was going to show up. But show up, they did.

A handful of times that first night, the chandelier lights above our dining room table unexplainably flickered. MaryLou and the others who witnessed it were absolutely certain it was Heath saying hello. Excitement filled the room each time this happened, but I barely noticed it. I was too busy in my own sorrow to wrap my mind around the idea that he might be sending signs to us from the other side.

Besides, like I mentioned before, he was never, and I mean never, interested in anything regarding communication with the dead or the spirit world. He was a very spiritual man, but he'd never connected with those topics or anything different from what he'd been taught through family or church. I always thought this was due to him carrying that ominous feeling that he might die young, just as his father had. He worried about it deep in his soul. He shared that with me throughout our relationship, especially after his first accident. But it didn't come up very often because it made me too uncomfortable. The what-ifs were too scary to think about.

That being said, neither of us was naive enough to think it could never happen, and we would joke instead about how we expected the other to grieve if one of us did die young. We had a pact, and it would come up now and then, with the conversation going something like this:

Me: If you die young, I am *not* wearing black all day, every day for the rest of my life like all the other Greek widows, like your YiaYia does.

Him: That's fine, but you'd better not get remarried.

Me: No problem. I don't want another husband besides you. But you would definitely have to get married again. Your mom would need another daughter-in-law.

I'd laugh, and we'd hug and be happy with our promises to each other.

THE HUSBAND ON LOAN FROM HEAVEN

It was basically the exact same conversation throughout the years, especially after his first accident and brush with death when he was only twenty-seven. We both knew where our hearts were with this topic, but we were also assuming we'd never have to address it so soon. Right?

But that first night, in my bereaved mind, when the lights above the dining table flashed, I wondered, *How could that be? How could he feel differently about supernatural signs now that he has passed? Would he be able to send us signs? Would he believe in them now that he is on the other side? And how would any of us even know what to look for?* Granted, our lights had never flickered before in all of our years living in this home, but still . . . I chose to ignore it, ignoring what might have possibly been the first real sign from him since he passed. I look back now and realize how wrong I was.

There were other times that night when I could have paid more attention to what might have been Heath reaching out from the other side. But my grief was crippling, and I couldn't comprehend it. I couldn't think outside the box.

When I phoned our dear friend, Taja, to let her and her husband, PK, know what had happened, PK said he was coming to our house. When he arrived a short while later, he quietly pulled me aside and told me that as he was walking down the boardwalk to our house, he started talking to Heath in his head. He kept asking over and over, "What do I tell the boys?"

PK shared with me that, in no uncertain terms, he had absolutely heard Heath answer, "Tell them I'm with my dad."

Those simple words sounded just like something Heath would say, and they were so comforting. I told PK what Niko said about seeing Heath and his Bapa Bruce right outside the airplane window. These aren't things that Niko and PK would make up in their grief, and I knew that. But I still brushed it all aside. My mind was too heavy with waves of sadness to pay much attention then. As I look back now, there were signs from Heath *all over*, even that first night. I just wasn't quite ready to believe. And now I know with all my heart that this is the first thing you have to do in these otherworldly instances . . . you have to believe.

Heading to bed by myself without my husband was the most dismal ending to what I can only say has been the worst day of my life. Our sweet, gentle Smith cuddled with me for a little bit but moved to his own room, I'm certain, to cry himself to sleep. My poor babies. My own shattered mama heart had no way to heal their broken hearts, and that hurt (and still does) more than anything.

Memories of losing Heath so unexpectedly at the hospital, having to leave him there all alone on a gurney with a breathing tube still stuck in his mouth, then going to bed and sobbing uncontrollably are still traumatic for me to even think back on now.

That first night, I was jerked awake countless times by what I can only explain as never-ending panic and deep, dark heartache. Then, as I woke up by myself in our bedroom Saturday morning to the realization that Heath would never lie next to me again, it didn't feel real. I didn't feel real. Life wasn't real. And all the while, I was wondering, always wondering, *How did this happen? Why him? Why us? Why?*

My pure gut instinct when trying to come up with an answer for *why* or *how* this had happened to such an incredible skier like Heath led me every time back to his vaccination only days earlier. From the moment I heard about the accident, as I was standing in my bathroom with wet hair and a towel wrapped around me, my wheels had been turning, and my brain had been trying to wrap itself around how this could have happened. Heath and I had been following the news, and it had been reported over the past few weeks that some of the vaccines were shown to cause brain bleeds, heart attacks, and more.

Immediately, I knew in my heart that as soon as I saw his autopsy, it would show he'd had a brain bleed. Of course, the twig that broke through his Arc'teryx ski jacket, long johns shirt, and, finally, his chest was likely the ultimate cause of his passing. But I knew without a shadow of a doubt that he had headed into that tree because he wasn't feeling well from what was likely a brain bleed due to the vaccine. I couldn't wait to get my hands on his autopsy to confirm what I suspected. I knew there was no way to prove to a pharmaceutical company that it had led to my husband's death, but I needed to know for myself. This is not my way of opening a can of worms and asking you to defend your own health choices. This story is mine and Heath's. It's also the story of how the vaccine helped end his life. Please know that I feel strongly that many people, especially the elderly, have benefited from getting vaccinated. My own mom and MaryLou have taken all their doses and have not noticed any negative effects. It is what it is. But I knew from the minute I heard how Heath hit a lone tree at only about five or six miles an hour that the vaccine likely contributed to my husband's loss.

It would take four long, drawn-out months to get that autopsy report, and I will share more about it in a later chapter. As days and weeks went on, though, I began to meet new widows with similar stories, and it was heartbreaking to know that maybe, just maybe, we could have had more time with our husbands if they had not chosen to get vaccinated.

Saturday Morning

The next morning, I heard a light knock on our front door and opened it to find my friend Marie and her daughter, Andrea, standing on my porch. I couldn't have picked a better pair to greet me that first day.

Marie's husband, Ken, had died of an aggressive cancer less than a year before. She and Andrea knew exactly how I felt. They pulled me into a big group hug, and a few tears flowed between the three of us. People who *get* grief just get it. I was so grateful to have someone there who understood exactly how I felt. As they shared their condolences, Andrea handed me a basket of bagels, cream cheese, and Starbucks coffee that would undoubtedly feed all the people who would soon fill our home again to gather and grieve.

Marie told me something important that morning that has stuck with me ever since, and I've shared it multiple times with other grieving widows. "Say *yes*. Say *yes* to all the ways people will want to love and support you during this time. Let them pray for you, bring you a meal, take your dogs on a walk, or sit with you. And don't take anything personally. People don't know what to say or do for us, but we need to give them grace with their words and their actions because a lot of them are hurting, too."

I took her advice to heart from that first day. When other new widows reach out to me now, I share Marie's advice and remind them that everyone has a different way of grieving—and different ways of helping or supporting their family and friends. For some, it's cooking a wonderful meal. For others, it's picking up your kids from school. For another, it might be sending a house cleaner your way to take that chore off your plate.

One more crucial lesson I learned that first post-traumatic day home is that I could not handle all the texts and calls coming in by myself. It was overwhelming to have to think about anything besides my grief and my kids. I didn't want to talk to anyone unless they were standing right in front of me. And even then, I still didn't want to talk to anyone other than a handful of people. I just did not have the stamina. And truthfully, I just didn't care sometimes.

I didn't care what was being served for dinner, who was stopping by, or what flowers were being delivered. I just did not care. I was grateful, sure—so grateful. But none of those things mattered to me. I had just lost my person. And I had just lost myself.

Thankfully, Laurie gracefully stepped in through her own heavy grief and kept life as balanced as she could for us. She let people know when we felt like having company over or food dropped off and, on the other hand, when we just didn't have the energy for visitors. Our village came together during this unexpected and trying time, leaning on each other as they all processed what had happened to one of their own.

Later that first morning, Laurie drove the kids and me to the hospital to say goodbye to their dad. I remember Niko playing Eminem's "Lose Yourself," one of Heath's favorite hype songs that he would play when we were driving to ski races and trying to pump up the kids at 6:30 in the morning. It was the perfect choice for the car ride and helped keep our minds off the upcoming difficult task at hand.

Laurie waited in the car while we said our goodbyes, once again my angel on Earth whom I needed during such a painful time.

I don't recall our walk into the ER, but I likely blocked it out because my walk in there the day before had turned out so horribly wrong. I do remember the dreadful, nauseous feeling I had deep in the pit of my stomach from knowing I was about to witness one of the most heart-wrenching scenes one could imagine . . . your children seeing and touching their beloved father for the last time.

Chaplain Paul greeted us warmly and escorted us to a hospital room where he said Heath was laid out on a bed for us to visit. Before entering the room, the chaplain pulled me aside and said, "Kelsy, I've never seen anything like this, but I wanted you to know before you go in. One of your husband's eyes is open. I know you closed them yourself yesterday in the operating room. And last night, I checked on him again before I left for the evening. His eyes were still closed. This morning, though, one bright-blue eye is wide open. Would you like me to place a penny there to cover it so it doesn't upset you and the kids?"

I couldn't help myself, and I giggled. This was Heath. This was so Heath, messing around with us like he always did, pulling little pranks and being silly, even from the other side. It couldn't have been a more perfect sign—a God-wink from him. I knew without a shadow of a doubt that it was a sign from him, just for his wife and children. Even in my deep sorrow, I felt a fleeting moment of joy, realizing that my husband might still be connected to us in some way or another.

"No, Chaplain Paul," I replied confidently. "I'm pretty sure this is Heath wanting us to see him and his open blue eye. It will be fine."

The chaplain stood by while I explained what happened to the kids. Then Niko went into the room first, by himself, to say his goodbyes. Just knowing we'd see one of his beautiful blue eyes one more time helped make walking into the room a tiny bit lighter.

While I waited in the hallway with the other two kids, Smith fretted about whether he should see Heath. I left it up to him, knowing that pushing him either way would not be the answer. I was secretly glad he finally chose to stay outside in the hall.

MaryKate had her own private time with Heath. Then she, Niko, and I said our goodbyes together, holding Heath's hands while a kind nurse kept Smith company.

It might sound weird or even macabre to others, but MaryKate and I both took some photos of Heath while we said goodbye—my hand holding his with his wedding ring in its rightful place, his bright-blue eye with the little speck of brown in it, his strong, athletic body, and his handsome face as we remembered it. I wanted to be able to look back and remember every detail I could, and I'm so grateful for those last few, final, and precious photos of him.

I knew this would be the last time I'd be able to touch my husband. So I asked the kids to go back in the hallway with Smith and the chaplain so I could have a few private minutes to hug Heath goodbye. I crawled onto the hospital bed and laid myself partially on top of him. I snuggled my face up to the crook in his neck and felt his cold skin and the stillness of his body against mine. His body was so cold and unmoving that it was alarming. I just wanted to hug him, warm him up, and bring him back home. I lay there for a few minutes, my body draped on top of his left side, and cried and cried, promising him out loud that I would take care of our babies the best I could.

The drive home was a somber one. As we sped down the highway toward home, Smith began to worry, upset with himself that maybe he should have gone in to see his dad. He wanted us to turn around, but it was too late. I knew his first inclination to not see Heath in that way was what Smith needed. He needed to think of his dad as he remembered him from just a day and a half before—the strong, healthy father who loved him so deeply.

Night Two

T he rest of the day was just like the night before. Our living room and kitchen began to fill with people. Huge stacks of paper plates and plastic utensils were at the ready for anyone who needed a snack or meal, and love just poured out of the community to our family. It was like a glue that held us together. The fabric of our family and friendships woven together like a quilt to make us feel warm and loved during such a difficult time.

I looked down at my phone at one point that evening and scrolled to the last text from Heath. It was from just the night before he died—Thursday, March 11. He was getting ready to drive to the mountain and meet Jared, and I'd stayed back with Smith so he could go to school the next day. Smith hadn't been able to find any friends who wanted to hang out that particular afternoon, and he was excited to build a fort on our property for shooting pellet guns. I had been planning to go on a long walk by myself but saw how badly he wanted to get started on his fort. So I told Heath we would be doing that until dinnertime. An hour later, I sent him a text showing a smiling Smith with the beginnings of a fort.

Heath's text back—his very last text to me—read, *Thank you for going with him! You're the best mom!!*

My husband couldn't have sent a more perfect message for me at a time when I would end up needing it the most. Becoming an unexpected widow and a single parent are two of the most difficult transitions a person can go through. That text reminded me then, and continues to remind me now, that I can handle this. I can handle anything that comes my way, especially regarding our children. I'm so incredibly grateful for that brief but meaningful exchange with him.

As darkness approached that evening, I knew I couldn't go to sleep by myself again in our empty bed. Laurie understood and stayed by my side, night after night, for weeks, to help me feel safe in my own bedroom. We would just sob and sob together before falling asleep. It was such a painful but necessary time to connect in our sadness. When Laurie wasn't able to stay, my sister Jaimi or my friend Taja would step in for the night, grieving and crying with me as we dozed off.

As news of Heath's accident traveled through both our Schweitzer ski community and our hometowns of Spokane and Liberty Lake, dozens of baskets and vases of colorful flowers and plants soon began to fill the house as well-wishers sent their love and support from all directions. I expected that. I expected the flowers. What I didn't expect, but realized within just a few days, was that I couldn't keep them all alive. Honestly, it was just another reminder that I wasn't able to keep my husband alive. It was a trigger moment for me, seeing these bouquets die on my watch, and I knew I had to do something about it to stay afloat. I could barely take care of my broken self during those first weeks and months, let alone manage to care for living plants and flowers.

One of the best things I did was ask my florist friend Andrea (who was delivering many of our arrangements from her boutique, Adorkable Gifts, in Liberty Lake) if she could spread the deliveries out more. She had already thought about this and taken it upon herself to handle the delicate situation, letting the sender know each time that their flowers would be delivered as soon as possible but maybe not that particular day.

Those heavy, heartbreaking days felt like years every time I woke up without Heath by my side. There were many, many times when I became a little delusional, to be honest, in my early grief.

Maybe tomorrow he'll be here when I wake up, I'd think. *Maybe today he'll just show up like nothing ever happened.*

These twilight zone moments were such a surreal experience, prompting my traumatized brain to want to believe that little voice in the back of my head that would whisper to me, *He can still come back. This isn't really real.*

I'd lie in bed in the morning and look over to the bathroom door, just praying with all my might that he would miraculously show up and do his little "just out of the shower" dance for me, just like he had day after day for years. We'd laugh and laugh every single time, mostly because he was swinging his naked package around, and it was hysterical. He was always making us laugh, and pranks were definitely part of his arsenal. A few times while I was recording my podcast sessions, he even mooned me through my office window! His mom was the easiest target for him. She believed anything he told her, even if there was no possible way it could make sense. Sometimes, he'd let it go for days before he'd tell her the truth. Such a comedian.

If I ever needed a reminder that he was truly gone, every sympathy card and gift arriving at the house was a big enough sign that basically shouted, "No, he is not coming back!"

That being said, it is beautiful how people express themselves differently when it comes to displaying their love and support after a loss. We received many thoughtful gifts, including some of my favorite glassybaby candles, each representing a heartfelt word or phrase, like "Above the Clouds," "Strength," "Angel," and "Friendship." Several people sent personalized items, like a front porch lantern, glass vase, and wind chimes, all etched with Heath's name or a poem about love and loss. Neighbors sent gift cards for massages for me, and others paid for house cleanings. Some sent meaningful jewelry to me, and our children also received gifts like personalized keychains, bracelets, and more. The amount of love pouring in from the community to our family was incredible.

Local friends and family made sure we had lots of food to eat, but it was hard to keep up with the meal train set up to feed us. So many people wanted to help. I have always loved to support local businesses, so I asked Laurie if she could let people know that gift cards to some of the nearby restaurants might be easier for us to manage since our freezer was already full of ready-made meals.

I remember lying on my bed, hiding from everyone, when it dawned on me that a miracle had happened earlier in the week. It had to have been a miracle that I didn't need that breast biopsy on Monday. I'd had an MRI, a mammogram, and an ultrasound, all showing images that proved surgery was necessary. But that day, the surgeon saw nothing alarming.

God knew He was taking Heath home in just a few days and that the last thing I'd be able to handle was worrying about a biopsy result.

What a gift.

Widowhood 101

On Monday, March 15, I shared on my social media about Heath's accident. Because I'd already posted bits and pieces of myself and our family life over the years on Instagram and Facebook, it was important for me to continue to share my new journey as a widow on these platforms. Five years earlier, when I began hosting my events and podcast under the brand BLOOM mom tribe, I used social media to share much of that work. Being able to continue sharing my authentic stories and those of other women ended up being a form of therapy for me.

People sent grief journals as gifts early on, but I didn't use any of them. Instead, I allowed myself to be raw and vulnerable with my Instagram posts. That account basically became my own journal of sorts and still is.

I look back now to my Friday, March 12, Instagram post and still can't believe what I wrote, not knowing that I would be without my incredibly supportive, loving husband in just a matter of hours.

Flashback to last weekend in #nola where I had one of the best times of my life! Here's the recipe for fulfilling some of your own bucket list items:
- Believe in yourself and your ideas
- Have a partner who supports you
- Toss in amazing friends who cheer you on
- Mix with love, humor, adventure, faith, hope, and a dash of unknown

---

For days after Heath passed, I continued calling friends and family to break the sad and unexpected news. I also called his favorite clients, many of whom we were as close to as family. I've never been a phone call person because I like to have face-to-face conversations instead, but these were part of my death duties now, and it had to be done. It's amazing how much emotion you can expend in just one phone call. It was exhausting. Utterly exhausting, but necessary. And Heath was very fond of his clients. Some even got the privilege of knowing I called him Scooby! Many of them had worked with him for almost thirty years.

When we'd been married just a couple of years, he was looking for something meaningful to send to his top clients for the holidays. He liked my idea of sending a box of See's chocolates with a handwritten card. It would end up being the perfect way to show his appreciation to those clients each year for trusting him with their finances. These people deserved to hear from his wife. His widow.

All of those calls, and every death duty, as I call them, were triggers for my grief. I have never cried so hard as I did that first year. Huge, horrible tears accompanied by wails of despair that didn't even sound like they could come from a wild animal, let alone a person like me. I would not wish this kind of sorrow on my worst enemy.

Speaking of animals, it was very apparent that our three dogs were also in mourning. Rocky, our nine-year-old chocolate Lab, wouldn't leave a certain spot by our front entryway, and he would usually come into the living room only if our godsister Lina was over or Niko was home from college. It saddened us, but it was hard to coax a stubborn, grieving eighty-five-pound dog into doing what we wanted him to. He had been Heath's boy, running along on bike rides with him for years, and it was clear he was missing him immensely. For the next two years, Rocky rarely left his bed by the front door. It was as if he was keeping watch over us and the house.

Amidst my profound grief, I had so much work to do, and it was overwhelming to manage with the lack of sleep and stress I was under. I had to pull together any of the energy I could muster that first week just to take care of

Heath's funeral arrangements. Thankfully, Laurie and Lina were there to help me with the daunting task. The sheer weight of what needed to be done to make it a beautiful day that would represent my husband felt so heavy. Looking at caskets, choosing music and poems, picking out pallbearers, deciding on his final outfit—it was all too much for me, and I knew I needed someone to be with me to keep me calm and centered. In the end, the three of us agreed on the beautiful mahogany casket that looked as classic and strong as my husband had been. It even had a light-blue satin lining to match his eyes, and I knew that it would look amazing with the dark-blue suit I had picked out for him to wear.

I was happily surprised when I met the young mortician at the funeral home and learned that her name was Kelsey. She asked what Heath's favorite music was, and I told her we'd loved to listen to Dave Matthews Band together. She assured me that while he was in her care, she would have Dave playing in the background. I loved that idea and felt like we were in good hands.

A couple of days later, Kelsey called to request that Heath's burial outfit be dropped off. I stood in our closet that morning and looked around, wondering what would feel special to him, to me. I had already set aside his blue suit, a white shirt, a favorite tie, and some light-brown loafers. Opening his sock drawer, I recognized right away what pair I wanted him to wear. It was a pair I had given him and all three children just the Christmas before—a custom pair of socks with the faces of our three dogs on them. It made me giggle to see them. It felt so right to include our dogs—Rocky, Ouzo, and George—in this special outfit.

Next, I pulled open his underwear drawer, looking through it for what I knew would be the perfect set of boxer shorts. It was the very same pair his late Greek grandfather, George Menegas, had worn many years earlier. Throughout our relationship, Heath would pull these boxers out, but mainly only for big moments or special occasions because they were so well-loved and well-worn. Whether interviewing for a job, meeting a new client, getting dressed on our wedding day, or throwing on clothes on the days our children were born, Heath would lovingly put on those thin, worn-out, light-blue boxers with white trim.

They were the perfect addition.

The only thing left to complete the outfit was his deodorant. He never wore cologne as an adult, so the fresh lavender, piña colada, and breezy island vacation scent of his Fiji with Palm Tree deodorant was what most of us would think of when we thought of him. I tucked the stick of clear (of course it was clear!) Old Spice deodorant in the box next to his dress shoes, socks, and boxers and hoped that the next time I saw him, he would look as handsome as ever and smell like a tropical breeze.

It had already been such a long week for me emotionally that I asked Laurie if she wouldn't mind driving Heath's belongings to the funeral home. Once again, she stepped up for me like she always does. When she stopped by my house later, she admitted that she cried along the way, talking to Heath and telling him she would do her best to watch over our family and me. I couldn't ask for a better person to be my best friend.

Handing over the items that I wanted him—Laurie's dear friend who was more like a brother to her—to be buried in was heartbreaking for her, and she told the funeral home director to take good care of Heath and make sure he had his very favorite boxer shorts. God knew I needed Laurie when he brought her into my life (and Heath's) almost forty years earlier.

The next morning, I had a previously scheduled appointment with a doctor I had been waiting several months to see. Even though it had been less than a week since Heath's accident, I didn't want to cancel and be put on the schedule even further out, so I did my best to look like a normal human being and drove downtown to the doctor's office for my consultation. I hadn't really left the house since he passed except to go to the funeral home, so I felt like I was in a movie, watching every move I made from outside myself. It was a very odd, unattached feeling.

As soon as I started filling out the paperwork, I saw that I had to choose my marital status after my name. Insert gut drop.

Married.

Single.

Divorced.

Widow.

The word *widow* jumped out at me from the page, and I burst into giant, unstoppable tears. This was the first time I had to define myself as a widow on paper. It wasn't fair. I didn't even get to choose. This nasty new title was chosen for me. But in my head and heart, of course, I was still married. It ached like someone had just ripped a band-aid off a gaping, raw wound. I cried and cried, completing the paperwork as best as I could through my tears. I'm sure the man next to me waiting for his appointment thought I was nuts, but I could not control my sorrow.

But then, something beautiful happened to me that morning. I met Brittany Martin. Brittany was the darling young nurse in charge of checking my health information before the doctor came in. I apologized to her because I couldn't stop crying and explained why. She said she understood and then shared with me that she and her husband had recently lost their ten-week-old infant son,

Cal. After sharing a heartfelt hug, I commented on how pretty her necklace was, and she explained that it was in memory of Cal. She and her husband had necklace charms made with a small heart shape missing in them. The metal hearts were cut out of the charms and then placed in the casket with their baby boy. The charms were left with the cutout form of the heart, then put on chains for Brittany and her husband to wear and look at any time they wanted to think of their sweet little boy.

It was exactly the task I needed to motivate me to pick myself up off the floor and dust off my grief for a bit. I knew I wanted to do that for my family and friends in some form. It was like a new boost of energy for me, and it gave me a reason to keep going. A reason to get up.

I drove straight to my friend's jewelry store after my appointment and told him what I was thinking. Luckily for me, Sean Tracy and his wife Christie, have been friends of mine since middle school, and they knew Heath, too. So, they also felt his loss. It would end up being comforting for them to be able to help me organize my ideas and make such special pieces for our loved ones.

March 20, 2021

At almost the exact time that Heath passed away one week earlier, a vibrant and glorious rainbow showed up right between our house and his mom's. Our neighbors from all around the lake began texting us photos and messages, making sure we got them as we drove up to Schweitzer for a quick memorial we had planned for Heath for the next day.

The craziest thing about this rainbow is that when our dear friend and fellow ski dad, Jim Joy, passed away in his own unexpected ski accident in Ushuaia, Argentina, a similar bright rainbow showed up over his house exactly one week after his passing, and Heath and I happened to capture it in a cell phone photo. Our Liberty Lake and Schweitzer communities took the news of Jim's death hard. Like Heath's, it was so unexpected and just didn't make sense. Heath and I grieved and ached for months and months over the loss of our friend, but still, it never occurred to us that the same fate could happen to one of us. That only happens to other people, right?

And now, to be looking at a rainbow that seemingly hovered directly between our house and Heath's mom's house at the exact same hour as his passing exactly one week later? We knew in our hearts it was a big, beautiful sign from Heath, and we took it as such, just like Heath and I (and many of our neighbors) took the first rainbow as a sign from Jim a year earlier.

Driving up to Schweitzer that evening for the first time since the accident, I let the tears flow while Taja kept me company. My older kids drove Smith and Taja's son, Preston, separately.

I knew it was going to be an emotional weekend. We walked into the condo that I had spent the last seventeen winters in with my husband and kids, and it hurt. My heart hurt so much. And it felt empty at the same time. The condo and my heart both just felt empty. The energy felt different. I walked down the stairs toward our bedroom and immediately noticed the pile of clothing on the carpet next to our dresser—Heath's pile of clothes, the same ones he took off the night before he went skiing for the last time and left on the floor for me to put in the laundry later.

I cried and cried. Taja and I just stared at the pile, feeling all the emotions. It was unimaginable how all this had happened.

The next day, family and friends were going to gather around the snow-covered tree that took Heath's life. Some came from as far away as Seattle and Oregon to join us. I took the Great Escape up to the top of the mountain with Taja, and, as I got off the chairlift, I saw people arrive on their skis and form a group. I don't remember who, but someone asked me what I thought about the tree as soon as I looked over to it. They knew it was my first time seeing it . . . the lone tree that had cost Heath his life.

Of course, I'd skied past it so many times over the years, but I had never paid any special attention to it until now. I looked down the flat run and could not believe that that one skinny, little fifteen-foot tamarack tree (probably more like twenty feet when the bottom wasn't buried in a huge mound of snow) had taken my husband's life. I skied over to it, noticing right away where the twig he had run into had been broken off. Ski patrol had told a mutual friend earlier that week that they had broken even more of the twig off so no one else could be hurt.

Word had gotten out about Heath and the tree since his accident, and many skiers were stopping by it to pay their respects, see what it looked like, and even tap it with their poles as they skied by. He would have loved that and done the same thing, saying hello with a pole tap.

For a week, the common theory was that when Heath ran into the tree, the twig had pushed through his Arc'teryx ski jacket and punctured an artery in his chest. We knew from the ER doctor that an artery had been punctured, so that made complete sense. The problem for everyone trying to help him on the day of his accident was that no one saw the twig. It had broken off inside his body. From the outside, it just looked like a tiny brown freckle. There was no blood to help pinpoint where the cause of his injury was.

When he was placed inside the helicopter, they immediately cut through all his clothing and made an incision on his side to help them look for any internal bleeding. That's when his heart stopped. By the time they got him to Kootenai Health, they were just trying to get him to breathe again.

Niko had spent hours that week creating the perfect plaque to memorialize his father, and with dozens of people surrounding us in love, he and Uncle Jeff attached it to the tree. Friends, family, ski coaches, ski patrol, kids from the ski team, and more shared their support, love, and stories, then we all skied down the mountain together in honor of my husband. It was a bittersweet moment and one I'll never forget.

Later, dozens of us gathered at one of our favorite local spots on the mountain, The St. Bernard, and held a celebration, complete with speeches, music, and dancing. I'm grateful to the owners, Scott and Lea, for generously opening up their pub to us that night and the following year too, for that matter. Heath was always up for a good time, especially on the mountain (his happy place), and that's what everyone had each time we celebrated him there!

March 22, 2021

O n the afternoon of March 22, we celebrated the incredible life of Heath Robert Nickolas McHenry at Holy Trinity Greek Orthodox Church in Spokane. This is the same church where we were married twenty-two years earlier and where Heath's parents were married. The tradition started years earlier, when his Greek grandparents were married in the church hall by a traveling priest before Holy Trinity became an actual church. His Great-Grandfather Louis even helped gather money to help build that same church years ago.

Before everyone arrived at our church, I prayed intently over the little pieces of gold and silver jewelry I was going to hand out. I hadn't told anyone what I had been working on so it would be a surprise, and the small hearts, crosses, and charms had come out perfectly. Sean had crafted silver dog tags with the small cross cut out for our two boys. For MaryKate, YiaYia, Lina, Laurie, and me, he had cut tiny hearts out of round gold charms that I then added to bracelets or necklaces. I had him create extra cutouts of more small hearts and crosses to give to our closest family members and friends. As I handed each one out, I asked the person receiving it to pray over it and then place it in Heath's hands in his casket so he would have a little piece of their heart with him up in Heaven.

Cue the tears.

It was one of the best things I could do for myself and our family, creating one last, loving connection with him, even though I knew he wasn't really in that casket. I knew his soul was flying high and that it was just his earthly body lying there. Thank goodness, too, because he did not look like himself at all. To me, his face had too much makeup, and he resembled a gaunt cartoon character. This almost made it easier to look at him for the last time, say goodbye, and separate myself from the body in the box.

Father Daniel, who was somewhat new to our church, had never gotten to meet Heath, but he did a wonderful job memorializing him.

Driving to the cemetery, where Heath's family has a burial plot in the Greek section (yes, there is such a thing!), was like watching time slow down. Everything was going too fast, but time felt stopped, too. I know that might not make sense, but nothing makes sense when you're grieving.

At the end of the service, I watched the groundskeepers lower his casket into the ground, and I saw exactly where I will be placed after I die. I had decided at the funeral home the previous week to have his casket set into the ground twice as far down as necessary so I can have mine placed on top of his when it is my time. It was a decision I didn't make lightly. It made the most sense financially because it was less expensive than buying a separate plot for me. Mainly, though, I knew then, just as I know in my heart now, that it's where I ultimately belong—right by my husband— no matter what the rest of my earthly journey looks like.

Talk about surreal.

After the ceremony, hundreds of people joined us at Cody and Lina Krogh's home for a beautiful memorial. How they were able to put together such a meaningful event in less than a week is all about community and love. Friends and family worked tirelessly to clean, prep, and prepare, and I'm so grateful for the gift of the Kroghs, who are Smith's godparents, in our lives. Dads helped Cody with the lawn and flowers, and the ladies took turns baking in the kitchen with Lina and working on decor.

When Father Daniel arrived at the Kroghs' home, he prayed over the enormous amounts of Greek food and drinks. It was incredible to see so many of the people who loved Heath in one place under a huge canopy tent. With the help of audio and video from a friend, Mitch Williams, many guests took turns at the microphone, trying their best to come up with just the right words to describe the humble, hardworking, and playful man who had been larger than life and whose journey had been cut too short. Niko gave a heartfelt, poignant speech that blew everyone away, and MaryKate finished her speech by playing a song by Creed that Heath loved and made him think of her and the boys. The lead singer had written the powerful rock ballad in just fifteen minutes as soon as he heard he was going to be a father. When "With Arms Wide Open" began, MaryKate stood with our neighbor, Brogan, and the two teenagers began to sing together into the mic. Soon, almost everyone in the tent was singing along, tears streaming down our faces. The song, with words that mirrored some of our feelings, was the perfect release for many of us after such a long, sad day.

Our family still has yet to watch the video from that afternoon. It feels too painful to go there because it was such a raw day of emotions for all of us. I expect we will watch it together one day when we're all ready. But until then, I'm so grateful to Mitch for providing such a generous gift to us.

We ended the sentimental evening by throwing ceramic plates onto the Kroghs' basketball court, and this zany Greek tradition brought a lot of smiles to our guests as we tossed our profound sorrow and plates to the ground.

Looking back on photos from the cemetery later that night, it was clear to me that even then, Heath was showing up for us from the other side. In one photo, I'm standing with our children, just the four of us for the first time in a picture since Heath passed. Right on the edge of MaryKate's leg is what appears to be a huge flash of light. As soon as I saw it, I knew it was Heath, and others have since agreed. It was just another way for him to let us know he was still with us in some form or another.

Every evening, for weeks upon weeks, those same family and friends would file in, arriving with dinner or drinks or providing a meal that had been prepared for us. I can tell you I am so grateful for those nights spent together, the mood always intertwined with grief and love, sadness and even laughter as more Heath memories and Heath-isms were shared.

The next day, less than twenty-four hours after I buried my husband, I joined Niko and our neighbor and good friend, Tom, for an appointment with a real estate attorney Heath had just started working with. Tom had introduced Heath and the attorney to each other weeks earlier, but they hadn't met in person yet. It was now my job to finalize some real estate property transactions that Heath had left behind, and I was hoping that, with Niko at my side, I'd be able to get it taken care of and put behind me. The list of death duties was so long already, and I was well aware of all our financial and real estate undertakings. But now, being the one to deal with them on my own was a whole other beast.

I felt comfortable heading into the appointment with Niko and Tom by my side. But let me tell you, by the end, I left feeling like I'd been completely torn to pieces just a day after burying my husband. From the moment I stepped into the office, it was clear that this attorney assumed incorrectly that I was a housewife who knew nothing about our finances or real estate transactions. He made several comments about setting up separate trusts for the kids and me, and I was trying to understand how that worked. I asked him for more clarity, but I could already sense he didn't get me.

He replied, "You know, just in case there's a pool guy or something."

I looked at Niko and asked him, "What does he mean, a pool guy?" Then I looked across the table at Tom, thought about his daughter, and asked, "Is he talking about Brogan being with a pool guy?"

I shook my head in disbelief as I realized he was talking about *me*. Me. The unexpected widow who had just laid her husband to rest less than a day before. *What the actual hell is happening right now?* was all I could think. I'd thought I was going into this to meet a concerned, professional person who would help me through some of the hardest tasks I had in front of me. I did not expect to be treated like an idiot.

My voice rose in an angry tone as I explained to the asshat lawyer in no uncertain terms that Heath and I had a very committed relationship and that I was not some housewife whose husband did not communicate with her. I explained to him that I would not be remarrying a pool boy, or anyone else for that matter, ever. My blood was boiling, but I tried my hardest to maintain some grace. How dare he question me or my relationship with my husband? The only thing that calmed me down in that moment was Heath. I knew he had somehow stepped into the room with us because as I looked out the window past the attorney's head, I saw a huge white sign that I had not noticed when I walked in. I have absolutely no idea how I could have missed it! It was a twelve-foot-tall, ninety-six-foot-wide marquee on the roof of a tall brick building right in front of me that said RIDPATH. My heart rate slowed down, and I took in a big, deep breath as I realized what I was seeing. The Ridpath is the hotel, once an upscale Spokane landmark, where Heath and I held our wedding reception— our big, fat Greek wedding reception.

He was with me. I felt it immediately. I relaxed, still upset, but I thanked the attorney for his time and left that meeting room, never to go back.

Later, I explained to Tom over the phone that evening how upset I was with the attorney's words. Niko agreed with me that it was highly unprofessional and even downright rude. I did get a call from the attorney the next day apologizing for his behavior. It didn't make the whole situation any better. And, of course, I never did hire him. He probably didn't want me as a client by that time anyway, and that was just fine with me. I know he likely learned a lesson in it all, and I learned not to trust everybody I meet, no matter their title or profession, or even their connection to me.

They say people sometimes have a hard time knowing what to say to a widow or to anyone who's suffering from grief, for that matter. I never had that happen once, never, except with that attorney. Maybe that's why it sticks in my mind. Most of the people I've encountered who don't know what to say will start by offering, "There are no words." It's the perfect opening (and closing) when there is nothing more to say that will make someone feel any better.

I do know that most widows (and grievers in general) *want* you to talk about their person. We want to hear your stories. We don't mind seeing your pain, your tears. These are just reminders, even years later, that our person did exist, was loved, and still matters.

March 25, 2021

This was one of those days that takes your breath away, and I don't mean in some magical and wondrous way.

I had received a call from the hospital, letting me know they had more of Heath's belongings. I hadn't expected that. I'd assumed they'd thrown away his clothing, and I wasn't sure that was something I'd want to see. The woman who called reminded me that his ski boots were also in the bag, so I knew I needed to go pick it all up.

Laurie and I drove together, and we both knew it was going to be a difficult task with a lot of emotions. Just driving the same route from Liberty Lake to the freeway toward Idaho was so triggering for me, and once we neared the hospital, my body began shaking. We walked in the back entrance to the hospital, which made it a little easier on my heart. I never wanted to walk through those ER doors ever again!

We waited for a while, and soon, I was handed his green Rossignol ski boots, his ski gloves, and a white plastic bag full of his clothes. It was pretty heavy for just a few clothing items, and I didn't understand why until we got outside and opened the bag.

I hope you never have to witness anything like what Laurie and I did that morning. We took all his clothes and laid them out on the bag and cement to get a better idea of what we were looking at.

There was not a single spot inside his jacket, on his long johns or ski pants that wasn't soaked in his blood. The jacket looked like he had been mauled by a bear, and I am not exaggerating. It was shredded. The Arc'teryx jacket he wore was made out of Gore-Tex, so the outside didn't show a lot of blood, but the inside was soaked. I knew it was from the incisions on the Life Flight and that the team was just doing their best to get to him, but the number of rips and the amount of blood were unimaginable.

We both began crying, just realizing so completely everything he'd gone through to be saved that day.

I still couldn't help but think that none of this would have happened if he had not gotten that damn vaccine. I wanted to scream, throw a tantrum, and have the pharmaceutical companies see just what their vaccine could cause, but I knew it would be to no avail. I didn't have it in me to go after a big pharma, and it wouldn't have given me my husband back anyway. I *did* save all of his clothing in that bag for over two years, though, just in case I needed it for any reason. I finally threw it out one day when I realized it was just holding me back from healing.

March 31, 2021

One of the most beautiful sights I've ever seen showed up outside our dining room window on this day, and I know with all my heart it was from Heath. He was letting me know he was all right.

I was sitting at our kitchen counter, enjoying a glass of wine with his Aunt Gloria, who is also a widow, my former hairdresser, and a longtime family friend. I've known her most of my life, so she's always been Glo to me, even before Heath and I married. We were having an overdue visit, sharing stories about Heath and Uncle John (her late husband) and just connecting. Heath had looked up to John from a young age as a mentor in the finance world, and they had built a special bond over the years. I always described Uncle John as being as handsome as John F. Kennedy. And he had such a kind disposition. I always enjoyed him, and when he passed from cancer, it rocked our family because he was such a strong but quiet presence. As Glo and I sat chatting, I felt this strong pull to stop talking and look toward my glass dining room doors. What I saw can only be described as incredible.

Huge, larger-than-life, white angel wings in the sky were taking up most of the view in front of us. I interrupted Gloria with an "Oh my God, Glo! Look!" and ran to the doors for a closer look.

We both stood there, chills running down my arms, as I snapped a few photos of what I'd never seen before and haven't seen since. I knew it was my Scooby. To me, there was no other explanation for it. He had sent me another sign, and, just like the rainbow a couple of weeks earlier, it was just what I needed to keep going and have faith that I was going to be okay because *he* was okay.

That same night, a segment aired on our local Spokane station, KHQ, about Heath's accident. News anchor Stephanie Vigil had called me a few days earlier to ask me questions, and she did an incredible job sharing our story.

The amazing result of that single four-and-a-half-minute video is that it ended up being seen by people as far away as California and Arizona. More and more well-wishers began sending their condolences, and people I didn't even know messaged me that our story was making them rethink their relationships. Couples were communicating, and families were growing closer. It was a beautiful tribute to our love story, and I still see this happening to this day.

April 2021

Sometime around the second or third week after his passing, I was lying quietly in my bedroom, listening to music and trying to stop thinking about all the hard things. Fleetwood Mac's iconic "Landslide" started playing, and I burst into tears. The words *were* his accident. They were our story. Or close enough.

Heath had climbed to the top of that snow-covered mountain and turned around, into the tree. And it had taken him down. Now I am left to get older, sail through the changing ocean tides, and try to handle the seasons of my life without him.

It was devastating and beautiful all at once. I'll never hear this song again and not think about my Scooby. It's sad, but it makes me grateful because it feels like one more little connection to him—almost another God-wink. Even now, over three years later, "Landslide" will play at the perfect time, whether it's in the peanut butter aisle at Walmart on a particularly rough day, in my car when I'm feeling sad, or even today, while writing this book at the coffee shop down the road. It always comes on right when I'm thinking about him or needing some love and encouragement.

Because Instagram became more of a journal than just a social app for me to document my grief journey, I later took the most emotional, inspiring, and hope-filled posts and created photo books with them. Now, when I look back and flip through these little books, they are helping me write this story. They remind me of all I've navigated on my journey as a widow, single mom, and solo parent. I want to share some of them with you because they not only represent my vast array of emotions at the time, giving you a glimpse into real-time grief, but they might also provide some hope and inspiration just when you need it.

Instagram: April 9, 2021

It's been 4 weeks today.

4 long, horrible weeks that feel like a blur and a lifetime all at the same time.

I miss my husband so, so much. I miss everything about our life together. Literally, one minute, you're happily married, and the next, you're a weeping widow. Even if I feel married in my heart—I'm basically not considered married anymore. Doesn't that seem strange? To have that pulled out from under you with no choice but to accept it?

Widow. Not sure I'll ever get used to that word.

I'm going to tell you (because I figure you're here, reading this, so maybe you'd want to know) some of my favorite things about him:

- He was so loyal and trustworthy.
- Very hands-on dad with all three kids.
- Supported me and my dreams and goals. More importantly, he believed in me.
- If you crossed him or any of us, you'd know about it. No one and nothing could harm us with him by our side. He'd talk to you about it and let you know what he thought!
- His laugh, once he got going, would make you laugh even harder!
- His butt! I loved his butt! I called it his athletic ass!
- His ability to think outside of the box.

- His desire to do his best in everything he did, whether it was work, working out, or just life in general. He always wanted to grow.
- His gift for words. He had a way of writing the best cards to us, always saying something really meaningful.
- His love for adventures and wanting to share those with our closest friends and family.
- His strong faith.
- His confidence in himself.
- The way he loved his mom (he called her Madre) was beyond beautiful.
- His love of his Greek heritage.
- His sense of humor. A perfect example: His Instagram name was @keith_mcjohnson

Smith and I are headed to Schweitzer and will ski to the top of the mountain to visit Heath's memorial tree tomorrow. As my new widow friend, Elena, told me about losing her husband five years ago, "I picked up skiing after Chris passed away because being up high in the sky makes me feel closer to him." I like how she thinks.

Instagram: April 16, 2021

There's no smooth sailing for us right now . . .

5 weeks ago today, my everything, my partner for almost 26 years, the captain of our McHenry ship, skied his way to Heaven.

Here's what I've learned over the last 35 days:

- I can do hard things. And honestly, I already knew this, but this has definitely been the hardest thing ever!

- People want to help, so I let them. I say yes to as many people as I can who ask what they can do—and them helping me helps them, right?
- You can simultaneously grieve and grow at the same time. I'm growing. I have to, to keep us all afloat. I'm learning things I never knew I needed to know about real estate, finances, trusts, wills, etc. I paid the bills, but Heath handled all that other stuff because that was easier/his line of work, etc. There is so much to know—it makes my head hurt daily.
- I'm so thankful that my husband and I communicated about everything. We always knew what each other was up to, and the fact that we talked openly about things like his work and our finances has made it easier for me when making decisions right now. Moms—you have the right to know these things. Talk. Ask. Learn.
- I've learned that people, even in other states, are hearing our story—and it's affecting them. Marriages are becoming stronger, dads are spending more time with their kids, unhappy people are finding ways to be happy. I love how he could not only inspire his friends and family before, but continues to do so now with his angel status.
- I've learned that the only way I can survive this is to be strong, to remember how much we loved each

other and our kids, to be proud of the foundation that we've built together, and to know that even though he's not here today, I will see him again. I know he knew how much I loved him, and that makes my heart a little, tiny bit less broken.

- I've also learned about deep, deep heartache and that the waves of grief can be calm at times, and then turn into a complete shitstorm the next minute.

And I've learned to give myself grace, big, heaping loads of grace.

Instagram: April 17, 2021

It's a beautiful day to celebrate my husband.

In the Greek Orthodox tradition, a 40-day memorial service is held for the departed. It's actually only been 36 days. I'm counting, but we were able to hold it early so our older kids could be home from college for it.

The main takeaway I had from the service, for all of us who loved Heath, was that we should continue shining his light through us, along with shining our own lights. As Father Daniel put it, "Light it up, light it up like a bonfire!"

This was really fitting, as Heath lit up our world so intensely while he was here on Earth.

Instagram: April 18, 2021

Finding sunshine in the darkness.

The week after Heath died, I realized that I would never be able to go out on date nights with him ever again, and that hurts my heart. We had a handful of restaurants we'd choose from, and we'd go at least once a week when we could. And we talked. Lots of our family decisions were made around restaurant tables. And I know I'm surrounded by a huge village of friends and family who will always make me feel included. But I will not let myself be the 3rd or the 5th wheel. So, I thought about what I could do to make sure that our friends and family will still want to come over and gather, even without my Scooby here. I also wanted it to be something that we would've done as a couple at some point. So I bought a pontoon. Well, WE bought a pontoon. I'm sharing it with Jeff and Laurie. And I love it so much, and it makes me smile. Heath would have loved it! And, of course, we're naming it *The Santa Cristina* after our favorite pinot grigio!

In my darkest times, I will always search for the light. I have to.

Instagram: April 21, 2021

"Loving ourselves through the process of owning our story is the bravest thing we can ever do" — Brené Brown

I felt brave today. So, I went to Jimmy John's to get lunch for my son and me. And I realized exactly why I've been avoiding going places since Heath died.

Because people we know see me, and they're sad for me, for all of us. And what I learned after seeing two people in 10 minutes at Jimmy John's is that I cannot be in denial when I go places. Their words and their looks of sorrow for me are more than enough proof that Heath is gone.

I can't hide and pretend that he's still here like I can when I'm at home, hiding behind my wine and my village of friends and family.

I felt like a band-aid was ripped off of my pain as I walked out with our sandwiches because if people are sad for me, then this all must be real, and I can't deny it, deny that my husband is gone forever. And so today, I was brave.

But I cried on the way home from Jimmy John's, and that's okay because it's part of my story. We have to own all the parts of our stories.

Instagram: April 28, 2021

Can I tell you a secret?

I figured out that grief is a lot like Instagram. You can spend an hour or two going down that rabbit hole, letting it completely consume you. I wish it was as easy to unplug from the grief like it is from your phone. But, since it's not . . . I'm trying to keep the grief at bay when necessary. I can do that by steering clear of toxic people or triggering things. We all have the choice—to let our grief, anger, lack of confidence, or other emotions control us, or we can learn to control them the best way we can for ourselves so we can not just survive, but thrive.

Instagram: April 30, 2021

50 days • 7 weeks • A month and a half. Whichever way you look at it, it feels like a lifetime and a blur all at once.

Scooby—so many days and weeks have passed since we had date night, since we hiked with the dogs, since we kissed, since you walked in the door, since we talked about the kids, since we made each other giggle, since you drove off in your Land Cruiser to go to the mountain, since you danced your funny little dance for me, since we had wine with your mom, since we drove through Starbucks together, since we watched *Breaking Bad*, since I last felt safe. Or normal. Or like myself.

Instagram: May 21, 2021

I'm walking into the weekend . . . without my husband. Again. The 10th weekend without him. I'm learning to navigate my new path, but there are definitely cracks in the sidewalk. Big, deep crevices I'm trying to not fall into. Instead, I'll keep taking baby steps and know that he's walking right beside me, even if I can't see him. Tonight, I'll be celebrating and thanking some of our village of friends and family who helped so much with Heath's celebration of life and more! I'm calling it the Grateful Girl Retreat!

Me: I'm the grateful girl!

June 15, 2021

I did something that I never would have done if Heath was still alive. It changed my life. And it brought me peace, so much peace.

On this day, I saw a psychic medium, and I don't even know how I found her, but she was perfect. My heart had spent the last three months completely shattered, and nothing was helping me piece it back together.

Then I met Tesa Harster.

Tesa is a certified medium who happens to live only fifteen minutes from me. When I found that out, I quickly set up an appointment with her, nervous but excited to see if she might have some answers for me regarding Heath and his accident. I didn't know what to expect, and I took along Taja for emotional support.

When Tesa opened the door, I felt instant relief. She didn't look like some crazy person or a scary witch doctor like you might expect of people who talk to the dead. She looked more like a beautiful blonde Disney princess or someone out of a fairy tale, even with her hair pulled up in a ponytail. I could feel her calm energy immediately, and when she told me her teenage daughter was named Kelsey, I knew I was in good hands.

We got comfortable at her dining room table, with Taja on my left, holding her cell phone so she could record the conversation for me. Then Tesa asked me who I wanted to speak with.

"My husband," I answered quietly.

"What is his name?"

"Heath."

That's all she needed to hear. Her eyes were soon closed, and she seemed deep in her thoughts. Within moments, she said she could sense that Heath was coming through. I was so excited that I got chills up and down my whole body. I *knew* it. I knew he would show up for me, even if this was something he absolutely did not believe in or condone when he was here on Earth. But I was desperate. I was desperate to communicate with my husband in any way I possibly could, no matter how unbelievable or unholy it might seem to others. This was my journey and mine alone.

Neither Taja nor I knew what to expect or think as Tesa started the reading. She had explained before she began that she would tell me only what my spirit guides or

Heath (or any other loved ones who might come through) had to say. None of what she was about to share was coming *from* her, only *through* her. This made sense, and for the next thirty minutes, she was able to bring all that Heath wanted to say forward to me. I asked her to ask him certain questions, and he was able to answer me through her, much of the time with her not knowing what we were talking about because she was just the messenger.

It was unbelievable and mind-blowing, opening a whole new world for me that I never knew existed. To me, it was magical, like I was practically in the same room with him. Of course, I wanted more. So much more. I wanted him alive in that dining room in Post Falls, but . . . I was finally finding some peace.

Tesa has all six clair senses (psychic abilities) and has since birth. As a certified medium, she has been tested and proven to have clairvoyance (seeing), clairaudience (hearing), clairsentience (feeling), claircognizance (knowing), clairgustance (taste), and clairalience (smell).

She explained that she was a little surprised that Heath was coming through so clearly because he had been on the other side for only a few months. I was not surprised. Even on the other side, he was larger than life! It made me weepy to know he was still somehow him, even on a completely different level—maybe even in a different universe.

My first little heavenly chat with Heath was more than I could ever have hoped for. Toward the end of our session, Heath was very clear that I was supposed to look for something on his nightstand table in our bedroom. I couldn't think of anything significant about it, but Tesa said he was adamant that I needed to check his side of the bed. I was confused because I had already put away most of the things on his nightstand. Certain pieces of him (his glasses, etc.) were too painful to look at on a daily basis, so I had cleared his things and put them away.

When I arrived back home that afternoon, my head swimming with all I'd learned in my reading, I headed straight to our bedroom and went to his nightstand. The only thing on it was a small wicker basket that held a remote. I picked it up and looked inside. At the very bottom sat a small, smooth glass stone—the same stone Heath had chosen from a bowl as a keepsake when we were at the memorial for Jim a year earlier. That is exactly what he wanted me to find, and I knew it immediately. It was his way of letting me know that he was okay. That he was with Jim. I immediately got the chills (I call these truth bumps, not goosebumps, because they usually happen to me when something rings true), and I thanked him for showing me such an incredible sign.

Instagram: June 20, 2021

100 days

Happy Father's Day to my sweet husband in Heaven. You'd be so proud of us as we navigate our new norm. Thank you for watching over us the last 100 days, guiding our children as only you could, and being such an amazing example of a father and husband during your short time on Earth. I'm hugging you tight in my mind right now and am so thankful for you! Love you, Scooby!

June 21, 2021

This was another celebration of Heath's life that we didn't expect at all! Several people in our Liberty Lake community came together, unbeknownst to our family, and had a plaque made to memorialize him. The owners of Lorraine Jewelers, my friends Jerianne Foy and Rian Emmerson, Britney Edwards from Plush Boutique, and the mayor of Liberty Lake, Cris Kaminskas, worked together for weeks to gather funds from the community and line up a news anchor to record the special occasion.

It was the perfect little memorial because they had it placed on a park bench along a path I walk almost every single day. A beautiful tree had been planted next to the bench years earlier in memory of another Liberty Lake resident who had passed away, so it was fitting that the bench had become a memorial of sorts. The five of us (our children, MaryLou, and I) were so surprised by the presentation of the plaque and the gifts that were given to us. Something wonderful also came from that day—my new friendship with Lorraine and Naim, the owners of Lorraine Jewelers.

Instagram: June 26, 2021

We are celebrating a life well lived. Maybe it's me just always wanting to keep his memory alive (plus, I do like to throw a good party), but I'm so excited to see all the family and friends heading to our home today to celebrate and remember my beautiful husband. (Listen, he was my Greek god in my eyes!) His heart, wisdom, wit, charisma, and charm won me over 26 years ago, as it did everyone else who met him. (Unless you crossed him or one of us. Then, watch out!)

I made this day extra special by ordering birthday cake and little gifts for everyone at the celebration to take home. Stickers with a photo collage of him and keychain beer bottle openers that said, "OPA! Cheers to Heath!" added a festive touch to the day.

The neatest thing happened for our family today, too. It was Heath's birthday party, but we were given the gift of naming a ski run in honor of him on Schweitzer Mountain. Our friends, Tod and Val Whitman, had won a bid at an auction for it, and they surprised us with the thoughtful gesture. Now, a big, blue trail sign that reads HEATH'S VIEW sits right at the top of The Great Escape chairlift and near his tree. If you ever stop by the mountain, take a picture under HEATH'S VIEW and be sure to tap his tree with your ski pole when you go by!

Instagram: June 27, 2021

Today would be my husband's 50th birthday! Never in my life did I think that he would be spending it in Heaven, and we would be spending it here on Earth without him. I am forever grateful for the love we shared, our kiddos, and the life we have built together. Yesterday's birthday celebration meant so much to me because I wanted to honor him and the relationships he held with our family and so many special friends. It was lovely. And I am thankful, sooo thankful. And I am tired. I'm ready to just be and not be planning anything. I'm ready to just learn to live this new life without leaving him behind but, instead, bringing our memories along. The celebration yesterday was a final touch, one final Heath memory to add to our beautiful life together. Thank you to everyone who came, those who couldn't be there but cared, and all of you who have shown up for the McHenrys these past 3 months. We love all of you! Please toast Heath today with whatever sounds good to you on this, his 50th birthday!

Instagram: July 5, 2021

Grateful, Thankful, Blessed

Yesterday was one of the hardest days yet. The 4th of July has been so special to our family over the years because where we live is like a modern-day Mayberry. Parades, golf cart floats, decorating, entertaining, boating and swimming, opening our home to lots of friends and family, and just feeling festive!

But . . . yesterday, I threw myself a pity party for a few hours. I didn't see it coming at all, but it was like a bulldozer pushing in. So I let the tears fall, hid in my room for a while, and then got off my butt and remembered that Heath would not want me to be sad. So I rallied. And guess what? People ended up trickling in, I made lots of food, and it ended up being a blast.

Just a reminder to anyone else who needs to hear it— it's okay to have a bad or an off day. Just don't unpack your baggage and stay there! Life's too short for that!

Instagram: July 12, 2021

4 months

Being at the beach in Oregon this week has reminded me that grief comes in waves. Some days, there's no way to handle the storm that has been the last four months. Grief sucks. And it can suck the life out of you. But I won't let it. I will not let the grief break me. My husband did not marry a wimp. (Unless you're talking about skiing black diamonds, and then I'm out!) I honestly still can't believe this is my life now. I was sure we had another 35-40 years together, and wow, do I feel a little resentful when I see elderly couples. I can't help it. I was robbed of a future with my person. But, I'm reminded every time I look at one of our kids, or have wine with his mom, or hear from a friend who knew us as a couple, how lucky I was to have him for the time I did. Almost 26 years, more than half his life! So, I'm heading out to have a glass of wine at our favorite pub here and toast my Scooby!

Instagram: July 24, 2021

Today was one of those days that reminds you how good life can be, even for a new widow.

If you've followed my journey since Heath died, you'll know that a kind stranger reached out shortly afterward with a cell phone video that he took from the top of the ski mountain that day in March. He caught shots of the Life Flight helicopter that Heath basically earned his angel wings on. Sean Allen, his darling wife Rona, and their six children feel like part of the family now because of Sean's quick thinking to videotape that flight and the heart behind that action. As a previous emergency worker, he recognized the severity of the moment and knew it might be important to that person's family to have the video. It's really a beautiful video, with the helicopter taking off slowly, turning, and flying Heath right toward Heaven. It has brought so much peace to our family, and the Allens bring nothing but happiness and joy to our lives. I'm thankful that out of the darkness can come such a bright, incredible rainbow (in the form of 8 amazing humans we like to call the Allen Army).

July 27, 2021

Well, it finally arrived. The autopsy. That's not something you ever want to see—the official document that states exactly how your person passed. It's just so final, you know? But I was so sure of what I was going to see that, although it made me heartsick to look at it (the same way I felt when I received his death certificate), I tore that manila envelope open with anticipation.

I know that the twig ultimately caused his untimely death, and that was clear. It lacerated his left sternocleidomastoid muscle and perforated his left subclavian vein. And there were liver lacerations from the incision on the Life Flight. But there it was, the answer to whether or not he may have had a brain bleed, right in front of me.

"Diffuse but scant subarachnoid hemorrhage over the cerebral hemispheres of the brain."

Of course I went straight to Google to find my answer: *Bleeding in the space between your brain and the membrane that covers it. Most often, it occurs when a weak area in a blood vessel (aneurysm) on the surface of the brain bursts and leaks. The blood then builds up around the brain and inside the skull. This increases pressure on the brain.*

I knew there was no way he could have possibly hit a tree going five miles an hour on a flat run without feeling off for some reason. Anyone can argue with me all day about it, but he didn't have a scratch on his head, his helmet, or his ski goggles. He never hit his head on the tree. No concussion either. I know in my heart that his vaccination caused him to have the brain bleed—something that was happening to other people who got the vaccine, as shared all over the news right around the time of his accident.

Does it matter? Can I do anything about it anyway?

No, but it gave me clarity. Sometimes, that's all you need—to know the truth, even if not everyone will feel the same way.

Instagram: August 8, 2021

Heath's AURA showed up!

You guys! We were ending our last-minute mom's trip in Seattle and drove by our old house where Heath, Niko, MaryKate, and I lived in Wallingford. Heath was with me in this photo! You can see the rainbow around my whole body. I can't even explain it! Of course I cried because how amazing is that? It's been almost 5 months since he died. It still seems so unreal, so unbelievable, really—but these little signs keep me going!

Instagram: August 17, 2021

New episode

This latest episode of my *Mama's Gotta Bloom* podcast goes deep. I flipped the script and asked my friend and fellow author, Kristina Kuzmic, to interview me about my grief journey with the hope that it will help others grieving or wanting to support someone who is grieving. There are tears, laughs, and a lot of life lessons built into this episode. Walk with me from that first phone call I got telling me my husband was in an accident to how I've been learning to live with his loss for the last 5 months.

Thank you, Kristina, for cheering me on from the first moment we connected back in 2016. You are a gem of a human and an inspiration to me and so many others!

Instagram: August 22, 2021

23 years, almost

Today would be our 23rd wedding anniversary. Here are 10 reasons to love my life now, even without my husband, best friend, and protector by my side:

1. Niko
2. MaryKate
3. Smith
4. Family

5. Friends and our community

6. Traditions we started together that mean even more now

7. The family adventures we took that don't have to stop

8. The knowing that Heath loved me for more than half his life

9. The peace that comes with knowing I'll see him again

10. The thought that I got to be his and understanding that almost 26 years is a helluva long time, really (just not long enough for me)

Instagram: August 23, 2021

Choose joy

In case someone needs to hear this today, your joy is up to you. Imma repeat that—your joy is up to you. My husband is gone. My life as I knew it is gone and along with it, the plans we had made and the adventures we had talked about taking. I don't get to grow old with my person. I'm sad AF but . . . I'm choosing joy anyway. Yes, you'll see me throw myself a quick pity party here and there, but I will intentionally continue to choose joy because I only have one life, and I want to enjoy it. And my husband would want me to do that, too.

Instagram: August 30, 2021

Last week, my daughter asked me how I am so strong. I told her I don't have a choice. I explained that I am holding up our little world and our family all by myself now, and it made me realize how much my husband did to carry our family. And to protect us. And to provide for us. It's not lost on me that much of my widow and mom confidence comes from how confident Heath was in me as his wife, as the

THE HUSBAND ON LOAN FROM HEAVEN

mother to his children, and even as the encourager I am through my BLOOM work.

We *all* have choices every day. We can choose to be a victim, or we can choose to want to heal. We can choose to be a worrier, or we can choose to be a warrior. We can choose to be unhappy, or we can choose to be happy with who we are and what we have right now. Does that mean you should settle? No way! It means find your happy where you're at and choose to grow and bloom from there.

Easier said than done? For sure. But you won't know how strong you actually are until you try.

August 31, 2021

I opened our home to over thirty women so they could have a fun girls' night in, have the chance to meet my friend Tesa, and experience her psychic abilities. I felt so much peace after my first reading with her that I wanted others to be able to find that same relief if they had someone who had crossed.

Tesa did private readings that night for seven women who had lost spouses, children, or parents, and it was incredible to hear how she was able to bring forward their loved ones and share insights with them. If you are not a believer in communicating with spirit, it is important to know that I never gave Tesa a list of who was coming. She had no idea who my guests were going to be and no way to try to research them. She doesn't need to research anyone. She has the proven, innate ability to speak to the other side. I've seen it dozens of times over the past few years, and it's an incredible gift to receive. It brings me hope and encouragement every single time I have her read for me or watch her read for others.

It's important to share this with you because there are so many hurting, grieving people out there who wish they could talk with their loved ones on the other side. Tesa and others with gifts like hers are proof of that. When I see her help others, it just reinforces what I already know—there is more to this life than what most of us know or understand. Our loved ones who have passed are with us, just not in physical form.

Instagram: September 12, 2021

I'm finding the joy in the little things this season
6 months ago today, I never would've imagined:
- my life without Heath
- making decisions without a partner
- worrying how I'll hold our corner of our world up by myself
- what it's like to feel such deep sadness and loss
- how strong I'd need to be
- not recognizing my future
- being without my person all the time

I also wouldn't have been able to see how much:
- our family is so wonderfully supported
- my husband was loved and cherished by more people than we ever realized
- how strong our kids and his mom can be
- how resilient and capable I am
- how I can still find joy in even the simplest things

Instagram: November 12, 2021

8 months

When Heath left to drive to Schweitzer on March 11,
I had no clue it would be the last time I'd hear him say he
loved me. Or the last Thursday afternoon I would spend
with him. Or that the weekend before would end up being
our final weekend together. Or that I would soon have to
learn how to live life all over again. I've spent 35 weekends
without him now. That's 35 Friday date nights. And it's been

245 days of going to bed without kissing goodnight and 245 mornings waking up alone. And 245 days of me grieving, and also of me growing. Nothing prepares you for this kind of trauma. But what does help me is knowing how much we loved each other. We both *knew* we were each other's person. We'd joke that we were stuck with each other. And was it always perfect? No! But it was perfect for us.

If all you ever take away from my grief story is that you need to love your people, that will be enough. That will make me happy—knowing that I reminded you how important it is to show your love to your family and friends. To communicate.

It's easy to look back on the last 8 months and see only the sad parts. It's also just as easy for me to see the beautiful parts of this grief journey. I have no regrets because when my husband died, I know he died knowing how loved he was.

No matter who you are or where you're at, life can change in an instant.

Be the reason someone smiles today. Be the one to say "I love you" first. Be the one your spouse needs. Be the light for someone else going through hard times. Be the soft spot for your kids. But most of all, *be love*.

Instagram: November 22, 2021

Today's plan? Drink coffee and be awesome.

Lots of things on my to-do list this week, and I'm excited to get after it! Doing this adulting thing without my husband has taught me to be more organized, and also more flexible with myself. I'm only one person and can only get so much done . . . I'm learning to give myself grace when my to-do list doesn't get done as quickly as I'd like. The list will still be there, you know? But my sanity is more important than the dishes and the bills. So, for those of you stressing about all the upcoming holiday things you need to get done, this is your Monday reminder that although your to-do list matters, your mental health matters more. Take care of you first!

December 8, 2021

I hosted another gathering with Tesa, my psychic friend. It was an open house for those looking to connect with their loved ones before the holidays. I had shared previously on my social media platforms about Tesa and her abilities, and many grieving women had reached out to me, wondering how they could meet with her. My home was packed full of grieving women.

I have videos of these readings on my cell phone, but I will tell you there is nothing like being there in person and watching her do her work. There is magic in her messages, and when you see how she can bring forth souls to their people still here on Earth, it's nothing short of amazing.

The first woman Tesa read for that evening, whom neither of us knew, stands out to me. This was right before Christmas, and Tesa was able to tell the woman that her daughter had passed from cancer a few years earlier after many trips back and forth to Seattle for treatment. Christmas was her daughter's favorite holiday, and she loved putting up her tree. What clearly stood out was the daughter's message that she wanted her mom to decorate her tree and put it up. She was adamant about it and said, through Tesa, "Put the tree up, Mom."

The mother, already so full of sadness that sorrow radiated from her, burst into tears and admitted that she hadn't been able to put a Christmas tree up since her daughter had passed. This was just one of many spot-on readings that night.

My widow friends Allisyn Traber and Elena Zener were also there, and Tesa was able to share in detail exactly what happened to their husbands when they died. She also brought forward things that only these women and their husbands would know, such as a special song between Allisyn and her beloved Cody.

It was so beautiful to watch all these women hear from their loved ones and see the peace it brought each of them. I was intrigued when Tesa also shared the color of some of the belated souls' auras, sometimes called orbs. I hadn't heard of that before, and she told me that Heath's aura was green. She explained that it didn't have to do with anyone's favorite color. It was just the aura they projected. I knew then that I would be on the lookout for green orbs wherever I could find them, but I wasn't expecting much.

I was just beginning to get comfortable with communicating with my loved ones on the other side, anyway. It was all a lot to take in, even after I'd seen so much proof over the past six months of knowing Tesa and watching her work her magic with dozens of people. Little did I know what was in store for me. Within days, I saw the first sign that maybe Heath's orb was right around me all the time. Around all of us. And I saw that there are so many other ways our loved ones can connect with us, if only we believe.

December 12, 2021

I was sad, so I threw myself a mini pity party like I do sometimes. Then I decided to pull out my phone and look for any old videos with Heath in them. I just wanted to see him moving and alive, and I needed to hear his voice. I'll never have enough photos and videos. I wish I had more.

I make a little bit of a dork of myself by asking people if I can take their photos for them. I'll see a couple out to dinner or a family out somewhere, and they look so happy that I want them to remember the day. I'll casually ask if I can take their photo with their cell phone for them. Most people understandably look at me like I'm crazy, so I play the widow card and tell them, "I'm a new widow, and I just wish I had more pictures. I think you'll appreciate this later." They never say no after that. In fact, they are usually very thankful and gracious, and I walk away hoping I helped them by leaving them with a tangible reminder of their precious time together.

So, back to the videos. My mind was blown when I scrolled to the previous summer and saw Heath bouncing on our pool's diving board. He was standing backward, getting ready to do a backflip, and I turned the volume up louder to see if he was saying anything. What I heard still boggles my mind. A song was playing in the background on our outdoor speaker, and as I listened to the words, my whole body began to tremble. It was like he had picked the song just for me.

But how could that be? He was alive for almost a year *after* this video was taken, but there was an absolute connection now. I could feel it. I had never paid attention to it when watching the video that early summer of 2020. Why now?

Because this song would speak to me, and he knew it. He needed me to read the lyrics and hear the words. I cried and cried as I listened to Tom Walker's beautiful voice sing, "Wait For You" and heard the words, "I'm just prayin' you can figure this out; When there's nothing left, you know I'll still be around."

Our love was so strong and our bond so deep. I'll be forever grateful that Heath can keep letting me know he loved me and that he is still there for me, even on the other side. I can only believe in what I'm shown, and when I'm shown signs and God-winks like this, I will never take for granted the magic in his messages.

December 14, 2021

I t's hard to celebrate your own birthday, or anything at all, when you're grieving. But celebrate we did. I never expected to be a widow at the age of fifty-one, and trying to find joy in the heartache was something I had steadily been working on for months. I didn't want to be sad all the time. That's not my personality, and my sorrow had already taken so much of my life away from me.

I've found that one of the best ways to get out of my own way is to get out and try to have some fun. I was so excited when our good friend and real estate agent, Beth, invited a few of us to a Santa Clause Cruise on Lake Coeur d'Alene. Ever thoughtful, she had brought cupcakes and candles for me. After we'd cruised out to "The North Pole," the boat captain called out my name on Santa's List with all the other good boys and girls, and then the whole boat sang "Happy Birthday to You." Laurie videotaped me blowing out my candles. When we went to rewatch it a few minutes later, our jaws dropped. When I turned the phone around so everyone could witness it, we all saw a green orb dancing right in front of my face while everyone sang. It disappeared at the exact moment I blew out the candles.

It was him! Another sign. Another God-wink. It was getting easier and easier to spot him saying hi.

To help continue finding my happy, I scheduled a skate night the next day for all my family and friends. Heath and I had roller-skated at the same rink in Spokane Valley when we were in middle school, so it was only fitting that I spend a birthday there, even as an adult. Spinning around the rink with MaryKate and Smith, playing limbo with the Allen kids, devouring a cake brought by my mom, and watching everyone just enjoy themselves was a highlight of what was otherwise a shitty year. Celebrating my birthday there was just what I needed, and it was so much fun!

As the holidays approached, our family still needed to find reasons to celebrate, even though we had lost Heath only eight months earlier. For many years, he and I hosted a huge Christmas party at our house for our family and close friends. It is one of those annual traditions that everyone looks forward to, and we choose a dinner theme ahead of time to make it more fun. I knew this year would be an emotional one, but I also knew Heath would want us to continue the tradition. Just picture a smaller version of a Greek wedding (minus a bride and groom) with shots of ouzo, toasts, and Greek dancing, and you'll have an idea of the kind of party we throw!

Just a few days later, Jeff and Laurie and our mutual family friends, Jon and Lisa Sweatt, presented us with a beautiful and unexpected gift. The large, wooden work of art immediately reminded me of the Greek word *Meraki*, which means "to do something with soul, creativity or love; to put something of yourself into your work."

Ben Joyce, an internationally acclaimed artist based in Spokane, was secretly commissioned to create the piece for our family as a way to celebrate Heath's love of Schweitzer and to forever place his memory there (hence why there is a Greek cross placed at the tree that took his life). If you're familiar with the mountain, you would recognize Colburn Lake, too. Ben's primary focus when creating his art is to portray locations and the emotional attachment one can have to certain places. For this piece, Schweitzer Mountain and the cross representing the tree are both symbolic of where Heath is today—Heaven or *Heath's View*. What a true reflection of **Meraki!**

Our family has never owned artwork like this. We are in awe of its quiet beauty and beyond thankful for the thoughtful and generous gift from some of our favorite humans. It is on display in our ski condo at Schweitzer Mountain and is the perfect place for such a heartfelt gift.

January 25, 2022

I t took me a while to realize that Heath had found his own unique way of sending me messages from the other side other than that one time on my birthday.

My cell phone had a way of giving me a certain song in a video (like the pool song), or his green orb (not a typical circle like you might see when you are using your phone camera) would dance in another video. This didn't happen to just me. It also happened several times on Laurie's phone when I was with her, and friends who had heard about the orb forwarded me pictures of the green aura they found on their phones. Other close friends and family ended up getting their own signs from him, and it was so comforting for all of us.

If our dear friend, Travis, had any question about whether or not Heath was sending him a praying mantis as a sign that he was with him, he doesn't question it anymore.

A praying mantis shows up for him all the time, even now, over three years later. One even stayed at their house for a week.

Heath's cousin ,DeDe, who's been more like a sister than a first cousin, receives many signs from him. She and her daughter Tessa, along with most of Heath's Greek aunts, are quite intuitive and recognize messages from the other side when they see them. Heath used Lina's Alexa to play little tricks with the clock. Some people, like his best friend, Jared, have vivid dreams with him in them, and they're usually doing something together like skiing or just talking.

Once I recognized that Heath was using electronics to communicate with me, I began to look for more ways to communicate back.

One night, I was awake as usual at around two a.m. Grief is horrible for your sleep, let me tell you! I was wide awake every single night for at least a couple of hours, worrying and wondering about life, my future, my kids, all the what-ifs, and all the things on my very long to-do list. It sucked the energy out of me. But this particular night, I decided to turn on my cell phone and start recording while I lay in bed.

Now, I'm not telling you this was a pretty sight. Usually, I'm half naked because of hot flashes and have my night guard in. And I'm typically surrounded by clumps of used Kleenex, my eyes bloodshot and red from crying. But I will tell you that the first time I started recording a video in my room, Heath showed up. And he showed up big.

I started by asking out loud for him to show up.

"Scooby, are you here?"

I waited.

"Scooby?"

A glowing white circle appeared in front of me on my phone and flashed across the room. I was astonished!

"Scooby, show me again!"

Another white circle.

"Okay, Scoob. Show me one more time, and I'll believe it."

Another circle.

This continued as I asked him basic questions, like "Is it you? Is it really you?"

Each time, more white circles appeared. I would ask yes-or-no questions. If the answer was no, a circle would not show up.

And, no, these were not bugs or dust bunnies flying around my room. I can promise you that. They were white orbs, some crossing slowly in front of my screen and some flashing across faster, like a shooting star. I tried to see them without my phone, but they would show up only on my video. It was exhilarating. He was with me! I could feel it. I knew it was his energy.

"Are you at peace?" I asked.

One big circle showed up and seemed to answer the question for me. I breathed a huge sigh of relief. Then I asked, "Is Heaven beautiful?"

Wow. The answer to that question was nothing like I'd ever seen before. The only word I can use to describe the huge display of multiple white circles that crossed in front of me when I asked the question we all wonder about is *fireworks*. That's exactly what it looked like, and it was glorious. It went on for twenty seconds. I have proof. It's all on my phone, and it's just another reminder for me that even though Heath is not alive and standing in front of me, he's still with me. He's with all of us if we just stop and open our eyes and hearts. All of our deceased loved ones are.

As British author Roald Dahl (well-known for writing *Charlie and The Chocolate Factory, Matilda,* and other famed children's literature) once said, "Those who don't believe in the magic of the other side will never find it."

Finding ways to communicate with my husband doesn't take away the pain of losing him, but it does soften the blow a tiny little bit. It confirms that there *is* another place we go to when we die. I'm not scared to die now. I know there's more to the universe than what most of us can see, and I'm open to it now because I see how much my faith and his messages from Heaven have helped me heal and given me hope when I so desperately needed it.

230

A few days later, I received unbelievable confirmation that Heath *was* sending me those white circles every night. I was just sitting in our living room, finishing dinner, and I felt this pull to pick up my cell phone. I turned it over and saw on my screen a screen saver image I had not put on my phone. I recognized it because it's one of Apple's options, but I'd always chosen my own photos for my screen savers. This Apple image was a pretty sky-blue background with many white orbs all over it. The orbs were the exact same style, shape, and look as the ones I see in my videos when I'm talking to Heath at night. I *did not* have that image in my photo album and, like I said, had never used that screen saver for my phone. It also had a different time stamp than the actual time it was on my phone, which made it even crazier to see.

I was shook. But not shocked. Heath wanted me to know that it was him, and he knew I'd continue to need validation. The same thing happened again a week later—a different time stamp but the same screen saver. What a beautiful gift to see the magic in his messages from the other side again and again.

Around the same time that I began having my nightly conversations with Heath, MaryLou started unexpectedly waking up at three almost every morning. She would be sound asleep and then wake up and look over to her nightstand. Each time, the clock read 3:03, 3:13, or 3:23

a.m. She now affectionately calls this her coffee time with Heath because once she's up, she's up. She makes herself a cup of coffee or tea and just enjoys the quiet time with what she describes as his energy. She can sometimes even smell him. There are also many mornings when she will be having a particularly emotional time, and a bald eagle will land right outside her window. We're both certain it's Heath saying, "Hi, Madre. I'm right here."

March 12, 2022: One Year

One year. Three hundred and sixty-five days. Too long. I kept my mind off my grief by planning things—travel, trips, BLOOM events, cousin camp, girls' night out (or in). I am a better person when I am making things happen in my life. Of course, it would only make sense to plan a one-year memorial at Schweitzer to celebrate Heath.

I knew it was important for our family to honor him in a special way that was connected to our ski team, SARS. Heath had been involved with SARS for over fifteen years and even served on the board. My kids and I decided to set up a scholarship to support a few young athletes financially because it's such an expensive sport to participate in. Uncle Jeff helped by ordering special wooden signs that read HEATH'S VIEW, and we offered them to friends and family for $200 each. That money, along with more donations, went toward a Heath McHenry Scholarship Fund. We raised

$14,000 in just a matter of days! What a blessing and a testament to how loved my husband was by so many! That spring, I started to bloom again, and I think it was because I was ready to take back my life. I wanted to feel vibrant and alive again. I began planning for a new BLOOM event because bringing women together to share their stories, struggles, and successes has always been a passion of mine. It pointed me in a fresh direction toward this new chapter. Who knew that creating BLOOM six years earlier would help keep me encouraged and motivated, too?

I looked forward to posting on Instagram and Facebook and sharing with my audience, whether I was having a great day, just an okay one, or even a sad one in which I was crying and sharing my troubles. People were, and still are, incredibly supportive. Sure, there can be a few nasty ones out there, but that's to be expected. In general, from my perspective, I've found that most people are good and kind. And if they're not, see ya later, bitches! I have no room for toxic people in my life, and I won't let them in now, especially.

Many of my social media followers have come to feel like family and friends because they've been following along on my journey, even since before Heath died. They cheer me on, laugh at my silly stories, and many times thank me for sharing my story because it makes them feel less alone and gives them hope.

I've met and gotten to know in real life some of these people I've met online, like my dear friend and soul sister from Texas, Amy Berry. She had been following BLOOM for a bit, and when I posted on that Monday following the accident that Heath had unexpectedly died, she reached out because her father had unexpectedly passed away the day after. It's a different grief, but we connected on a deep level right away because these men were our heroes.

And the widows I've gotten to know who get me, well, it just hits different when someone understands your pain. We are our own unique village, that's for sure.

March 25, 2022

The days went by, and they were the same as always. I still cried myself to sleep at least once a week, a year later, and then woke up an exhausted zombie, wondering how I was going to get through another day unless I took a nap. It had been a whole entire fucking year. I was tired. I kept wondering what needed to change to help me move forward without leaving my husband behind.

The answer came in the form of a quick getaway. The godsista and I made a plan to go to Las Vegas a couple of months earlier to just unwind. We had no expectations except to have a great time together and enjoy one of our favorite bands, The Scorpions.

Lina *loves* The Scorps, and I knew we were going to have an incredible time in the two days we'd be in Sin City. All I wanted was to have fun, feel free, and feel disconnected from the pain and sorrow I'd been carrying for the last year.

Our little vacation was everything I'd hoped for. We shopped, ate, drank a little too much, and had one hell of a time—and that was all before the concert even started! Once we arrived at the Hard Rock Casino to watch the opening act, Skid Row (which is one of my favorites), I was in Heaven! I felt light-hearted, pretty (Lina did my eyeliner!), and ready for a fun night!

What I did not expect was to see a man there who took my breath away. We kept eyeing each other, and I immediately felt drawn to him. Soon, he and his brother and friend were right by us, dancing and singing along to the bands. It was like a magnet was pulling me to him, and I asked over the loud music if he was married. He held up his left hand—no ring in sight—and said he was divorced. My heart jumped. Let me tell you, that was the first time I'd felt an inkling of *any* kind romantically since Heath passed. It was a giddy, new emotion that I wasn't used to feeling, at least not during the last year I'd spent as a widow. I had been worried I would never feel that sensation again— being attracted to someone and realizing they might just like me, too.

The evening flew by quickly, like it can in Vegas, and it was obvious this guy and I liked each other. We ran around the casino holding hands and kissing for hours, and I couldn't believe I could have those romantic kinds of feelings again. It was surreal. I was just happy I could *feel* those feelings once more. I was still a woman. I was still desirable. I could still be attracted to someone and have that feeling returned. If you're a widow, you know what I mean. You don't know what to expect after your person leaves you. I'm guessing a divorcée might feel a similar way. That night kicked off a whole new chapter as a widow. Yes, it had been a year since the accident, but I'd not thought about another man since Heath passed. This man I met in Las Vegas helped me begin to heal and reminded me what I'd been missing. And, although we did not end up being together for more than a few months, my life changed. I realized how badly I missed my husband as my romantic partner, my everything. I had faced a year of needing romantic love from my husband but had been cut off by his unexpected death—stifled, if you will, with nowhere to put that kind of love and no one to share it with. I knew I was ready to find someone I could be romantically involved with again.

Breaking up hurt, but I was still so grateful to know that someone could give me butterflies again. It gave me hope.

Enter my daughter and her roommate! A few months later, MaryKate decided it would be a good idea to sign me up on the dating app, Bumble. I knew nothing about her bright idea until she and her roommate shared my dating app bio with me over a text message! I still laugh because she and her sorority sister were writing back to potential dates as if they were me. Of course, I was mortified! But it ended up being a fun way to spend lonely nights when I might otherwise have cried myself to sleep. It was a silly distraction, and I needed it. Talking online to guys and getting to know them was an easy way to dip my toe in the dating pool without having to meet them in person if I didn't want to. I did meet a few nice men and went on a handful of in-person dates in Spokane and Seattle. It was fun to get dressed up and find a reason to put some lipstick and a smile on.

The hardest part about dating as a widow is being vulnerable after everything you've endured. You're so exposed to the world, open, and raw when you are grieving. I had to learn to be aware of the scammers and the cheats. But I also had to be open to talking to someone and giving them a chance if they seemed like a good person and maybe even a good dating fit. It was a balancing act I got better at as the months went by.

And the stories, oh my! If you could see some of the bios on those dating apps, you would be shocked and amused. Married men looking for a secret girlfriend, open marriages, couples looking for a third partner, men looking for sex only—there's just a little of everything on there. You have to rake through the weeds to find even one good guy. Let me also mention how awkward it can be when you are looking for love on the same dating apps as some of your friends who are also widows, or single or divorced. I went on a few dates with a couple of ex-boyfriends from college, but it just wasn't the same. These were guys I adored at one point and still do, but I'm a different person now. I did meet one man who had such a beautiful soul, but he only wanted marriage in the future, and I knew I did not. I had made a promise to Heath, and it was what I wanted, too. I only wanted to have one husband, so we said goodbye and went our separate ways.

Spring 2022

"When you ask for signs from the Universe, the Universe speaks back." — Psychic Medium Laura Lynne Jackson

As the snow melted and the sun began to shine here in the Pacific Northwest, Laurie and I would take our almost daily five-mile walks together. Our walk is the same every day. I like the consistency because I end up at Starbucks for an iced espresso or a bathroom break halfway through the walk. It has become such a habit that it feels like a form of therapy. As our friend Taja has said, "I leave all my troubles on the trail."

It's such a cool feeling to look back and think of all the miles I've logged on that path by myself, with friends, and even with Heath before he crossed over. They add up to years of steps, years of growth, years of grief, and years of learning to love my new life even without my husband. He wouldn't want it any other way. Of course, I have confirmation of this because he's found a way to send me signs on my walks, too.

The trail is set along a golf course, and each day, I look for lost golf balls to bring back and set aside for Niko. One day, at the beginning of my ninety-minute walk with Laurie, I decided to ask Heath (in my head) for an orange or green golf ball to let me know he was with me. On our way back from Starbucks, we stopped at his bench—the one where his plaque is—and took our photo. As we stepped back down on the path, I looked over and saw a fluorescent-orange golf ball! My heart leaped, and I told Laurie what I had done. We just stared at each other in disbelief.

"He's here!" I told her, and we both smiled and kept walking.

Within minutes, a bright-green golf ball was hiding just beyond a bush, but I spotted it immediately! We were both in shock. It was incredible. There were no other golf balls to be found that day—just the ones I asked for. It isn't hard to imagine your departed loved ones in Heaven sending you signs like this once you believe it's possible.

You can brush the golf ball incident aside as a coincidence. At first, I might have, too. However, it's been over two years now since Heath crossed to the other side, and I can't even begin to tell you how many times this has happened again. Over and over, I'll ask for a different color, and we will find it. The exact color. Just that one ball. Maybe not that day, but the next one. One time, I said out loud as we walked, "Okay, Scooby, show me a pink ball or a blue ball."

As I came around the corner of the trail, I looked down, and there was one ball, just one, but the top half was a bubble-gum pink, and the bottom half was a pretty baby blue! You can't make this shit up! Even Laurie, who considered herself not super spiritual until Heath's passing, can't deny the crazy ways he has shown up for me, for her, and for many of us.

If golf balls and green orbs, shells, rocks and potato chips shaped like hearts, and other signs that I know Heath has sent won't lead you to believe in the magic of messages from the other side, let me share one more story with you. It's a doozy!

In April 2022, MaryKate, Smith, Smith's best friend, Preston, and I flew to San Diego for spring break to visit Niko, who was in his junior year of college at the University of San Diego. Luckily for us, some of our favorite friends and neighbors from Liberty Lake were also vacationing there at the same time. We met up with the Denneys (Uncle Jeff, Aunt Laurie, and their daughters Kate and Anna) and the Stewarts (Glenn, Debbi, and their son Alex). One night, the big group of us headed to dinner at one of my favorite Italian restaurants in Pacific Beach—Scuderie Italia—minus Smith and Preston, who were scootering all over Pacific Beach to their little hearts' content. After some amazing spaghetti arrabbiata and pinot, I was feeling adventurous, and I told everyone I was ready to get a tattoo. I had been thinking about it for a while and had decided on a tiny heart that matched the heart that was cut out on the necklace I had made for myself right after Heath died.

After dinner, the nine of us walked down Garnet Street in search of a tattoo shop. Within minutes, we found Above All Tattoo, and everyone was so excited for me. I walked in first, and, as everyone stood around me, I greeted the burly, tattooed guy at the counter and asked if they did fine-line tattoos.

Get ready for it . . .

The guy said, "That would be Skooby. He can do those thinner tattoos."

Insert a huge—and I mean huge—collective gasp from all of us as we took in what he had just said.

"Scooby?" I asked in astonishment as tears welled up in my eyes.

"Ya, his name's Joe Cordileone, but he goes by Skooby. You can message him on Instagram, and he'll be able to take care of you."

What the? What? Coincidence? No way. It was absolutely meant to be.

I messaged Joe immediately and briefly explained what I was looking for and the connection between his nickname and Heath's. He put me on his schedule for the next day.

What an incredible experience to meet Joe and hear that his nickname since high school has been Skooby. I shared more about Heath as he tattooed the perfect little heart on my left wrist, and he listened compassionately. He even took time to tattoo MaryKate with our family motto, *philotimo*, so she could match Niko, who had gotten his two years earlier.

If you aren't familiar with the Greek word, let me share why it means so much to us.

Greeks use the word philotimo (φιλότιμο) to convey a sense of pride in what they do, from small acts of kindness to supporting one's community to doing the right thing. Heath and I tried to raise our children with this ideology, and the kids and I continue living this philosophy to this day. Of course, we're not perfect, but it's a great standard to hold ourselves to, and it continues that connection back to Greece and Heath's love for his heritage.

Whether I'm walking my five miles on the beach in San Diego or along the golf course at home, I've learned so much more about the spiritual world and how our loved ones can communicate with us if we just listen. If Laurie or another friend isn't available to walk with me, I pop my AirPods in and listen to books on Audible.

The first one I landed on was written by spiritual teacher and medium Suzanne Giesemann, who is a former Navy commander. *Wolf's Message* is an incredible story of healing and love, but it also shows the world the impact that Heaven, and a greater reality bigger than ourselves, can have on us. This book opened my eyes to a whole new way of thinking. And it reiterated to me that Heath is definitely sending me messages from the other side.

Two books by psychic medium Laura Lynne Jackson— *Signs: The Secret Language of the Universe* and *The Light Between Us: Stories from Heaven. Lessons for the Living*— can also remind us that there is another, richer, and deeper layer to our universe that many are too afraid to experience. It's hard to wrap your mind around at first, but once you do, you can't look back. It's truly all right in front of you.

August 2024

As I write this final chapter, it's been three years and five months since my husband left this Earth. The hard life lessons I've learned over the last few years without him have been invaluable in keeping me on the right path. I've tried to carry the weight of my darkness with grace and grit. I could have easily let my grief take me down—take our family down—but my incredible husband would never want that. I know that as much as I know my own name. He would want me to *live*. And to *love*.

I have found, for me, that there is absolutely no reason to hold back love. I loved Heath big while he was here—so big. And I look back and am so glad I did because I have no regrets. I know he died knowing how much I loved him!

Grow Through What You Go Through

A little recap for those of you who like to read the last page of a book first!

Year one as a widow was horrible. Absolutely horrible. Honestly, it was hell. There was no way around it but to let the waves of grief crash over me as they came. Year two was also very difficult. But, year two is also when I finally started to see a light at the end of the tunnel.

I began to evolve. And yes, I am a different version of the Kelsy Heath married. I'm more spontaneous, more spiritual, and more connected to myself than I've ever been. I'm also now more guarded about certain things but more open in other ways.

I've gotten seven—yes, seven—tiny tattoos (several in honor of Heath, these special ones tattooed by Skooby), whereas he never wanted even one. I've had some upgrades done to our home to make it feel fresh, and maybe he wouldn't have chosen to do some of those new fixes. And that's okay. I'm at peace with most of the decisions I've had to make on my own over the last few years. It's not easy to become a single parent overnight and be in charge of everything—and I mean everything—but I've done my best to make the right decisions for our family. This entire journey has been one giant learning curve. Actually, it's been more like a wild roller-coaster ride, and I've been hanging on for dear life!

And this year, I fell in love. I don't know exactly what the future holds for us (none of us do—this book is a testament to that), but I love the path we're on! He's pretty incredible and has helped heal so many broken pieces of my heart. I'm so grateful we found each other (on Bumble, in case you're wondering). And yes, it's bizarre that I'm in love with two people at the same time—Heath in Heaven and Joseph here on Earth, but that's exactly what it feels like!

In this next chapter of my journey, all I can do is be grateful to God that He gave me Heath for over half his life and that by letting me have him on loan for those twenty-two years, I was able to become a mom to our three beautiful babies and grow into the person I am today.

No matter where *you* are on your journey with the death of a loved one, know that we all grieve differently and that there are no timelines for grief. I'm sharing this book and our family's story because writing it has been like therapy for me. I hope it will remind people, especially those grieving a loss, that grief and joy can coexist. But you know what, friend? You get to decide what works for you and how long and in what ways you want to grieve. I hope this book will ease someone's loneliness and pain by showing them there are others like them out here and that we are doing okay. And after a while, after a long while, many of us are doing better than okay.

Here are a few things I've done over the last three and a half years to help me get out of my own way when I've been feeling depressed or discouraged or when I just needed to set my grief aside for a bit.

- Walk! Get outside and get some fresh air! On hundreds of walks since Heath crossed over, my BFF Laurie has become my therapist. I never had to see a grief counselor because that is what has worked for me. Yes, I *do* know how lucky we are to have the friendship we do!

- Like the flight attendant says on the airplane before takeoff, put on your own mask first. If you can't take care of yourself, you can't take care of your kids and everyone else around you who is suffering. Don't let your physical or mental health slide. Get help in whatever way you need to before it affects your loved ones negatively.

- Lean on your people. If you don't have a community, create your own. Trust me, someone out there needs you, too! I've created a little widow group. We don't see each other often, but when we do, we are there for each other, even if it's just an encouraging text!
- Allow the new *you* to show up. Don't be afraid to share who you are, even with all the tears, trauma, pain, etc. Your pain is part of who you are now.
- Serve others. I've tried to do this as an adult, and Heath did as well. Help those in need, take popsicles to the hot and sweaty homeless, make Christmas cards for those serving overseas, and give back. I promise you that putting your focus on someone else for even a few moments will take the focus off your own pain.
- Be flexible. For me, this hit home when I had to acknowledge that our two youngest kids were struggling at school because of their heavy grief. I had to pick my battles, if you will, and choose what was best for my children, even if that went against the norm. Don't be afraid to make your own choices, even if they go against the grain.
- Share your story. It's amazing how many times I felt the nudge to share my story and found that the

person I was talking to (usually a stranger) had a similar story. Connecting is comforting.

- Embrace change. I've evolved through this unwelcome journey, and so has BLOOM mom tribe and all that it stands for. I'm ready for a new chapter that encompasses my continued growth as an author, a mother, a girlfriend, a spiritual person, and more. So come join me under my new Instagram name, BLOOM with Kelsy.

- Seek help. When Smith, our youngest, was understandably depressed due to his dad's passing, we had to find a way to get him the help he needed. Just putting him on medication wasn't going to cut it. Instead, we chose TMS (therapeutic magnetic stimulation), and although our insurance didn't cover it, he told me it was the best thing I could do for him. Think outside the box. Grief is not linear, and neither is our healing.

- Love your people. Don't forget to focus on the ones who are still here. That's it. Just love your people.

And a little P.S. (more like a love note to learn from) for those who aren't grieving a loved one . . .

Life is so, so short. I want to remind you that all the little annoying things you might think are big things are probably *not*. Dirty laundry on the floor, kitchen cupboards left open, half-remodeled bathrooms sitting unfinished—who cares in the big scheme of life?! Those are insignificant and will not matter when you get to the other side.

What matters is *love*.

And if, for some reason, you are left here without your person, you will realize that all those little trivial things add up to nada, nothing. They won't bring your person back. I would trade all the piles of dirty gym clothes, open kitchen drawers, unemptied dishwashers, and dumb disagreements to have my husband back!

Thank you for reading our story. I hope it leaves you wanting to love harder and bigger. I know I was put here to spread my light, so I'm going to do just that. I will not let anyone dim it because it is what makes me *me*. I'm going to sprinkle love, joy, and positivity everywhere I can, and I'm going to continue to live and love *big*. I'm going to continue to BLOOM.

XO

Kelsy

"There is no remedy for love but to love more"
— Henry David Thoreau

Acknowledgments

Thank you to everyone who helped bring this book to life! I'm so grateful for each of you.

Niko, MaryKate, and Smith—my precious babies. I never thought I'd have to raise you into your teens and adulthood without your beloved father by my side. You have walked this path with grace, and I couldn't be prouder of you. Your dad loved all of you so, so much. Please take the lessons you learned from him, the stories I've shared in this book, and the love I hold so deeply for you, and go confidently in the direction of your dreams. And always honor philotimo! I love you more!

Laurie Denney—Skitz, how do you thank someone who has been such a supportive and selfless best friend over the years? We've survived breakups and hangovers, bad grades and jerk boyfriends, health scares and deep loss, and every time . . . we're there for each other with a hug, an ear to listen, and a bottle of pinot. You are the yin to my yang, and I'm so grateful to God for knowing that I needed your calm to balance my crazy when he gifted me with our friendship at twelve years old! Thank you for being my beautiful bestie! I love you!

My mom, Diane Nelson—Thank you for always believing in me and doing your best as a single mom to make sure I had everything I needed. I grew up knowing I could do anything I dreamed of, and I'm sure much of that is thanks to you and Sweetie (my beloved late grandmother) and your love and support. I love you, Madre!

MaryLou McHenry—To the incredible YiaYia, who loves others unconditionally. Words cannot describe all the sadness and loss you've suffered, but you continue to show up for me, your grandbabies, and every single other person you love, no matter what! God knew we all needed you, and I couldn't be more grateful for our close relationship. Thank you to you and Bruce for giving me the gift of your son. My life is infinitely better because of him and you. Let's always be neighbors and drink wine! I love you!

My sisters, Jaimsyne and Merytt—You've both taught me different lessons as my big sisters, and you've always watched out for me. Thank you for your unconditional love and support! I love you both!

*Jaim—My life would not be the same without all the adventures you took me on as a child, the experiences you included me in as a teen, and the soul support you've provided me over the years as an adult.

*Mert—Thank you for bringing your three daughters into this world so I could adventure with them and their kiddos like Jaimi did for me! And thank you for not being just a great big sis, but always being my cheerleader.

Lina Krogh, the godsista—We may not be family by blood, but family we are. Thank you for all the love and support you continually show us; for the huge amounts of hummus, curry, and orange chicken that you fill our bellies with; and for being an incredible godmother to our Smith. You are so loved, and I just know Heath is up there getting ready to mess with your Alexa one more time! Love you ALWISS!

Tanya Goodall Smith—To my best-selling published author friend! I'm forever grateful that you invited me to the writer's retreat that started this whole process. Thank you for the years of friendship and the accountability piece that helped me through this when I got stuck. I'm proud to be on this journey with you, my book bestie!

Taja Ramsey—Tajatonic! Whether we are biking to drinks, walking to drinks, taking the golf cart to drinks (hmm, there's a theme here!), you have always been a wonderful sidekick and great friend to both Heath and me. Thank you for being one of my accountability partners in this endeavor! I hope our boys will always be best friends so you and I can continue to chase adventures together! Love you!

Tesa Harster—I am so grateful for you, your remarkable abilities, and your friendship. You helped show me (and many of my loved ones) that Heaven isn't as far away as we think, and you have opened up how I look at the universe. Thank you for the magic in your messages! Love you! (P.S. You can learn more about Tesa by listening to my podcast episode with her on *Mama's Gotta Bloom*.)

My girl gang (you know who you are!) and our village of friends and neighbors from Schweitzer and Liberty Lake who showed up from day one (March 12) for us—Thank you for the love, support, food, hugs, tears, gifts, laughter, memories we shared together with Heath, stories of Heath, and all the other things that have helped keep our family afloat the last several years. We love you all!

Sandy Scheschuk—I will always remember the first time we connected and how the universe aligned to bring us together. It has been such a joy getting to know you not only as an intuitive but as a friend. Your psychic gifts have continually shown me that our loved ones are always with us. Thank you!

Callie, Nikki, Kristi, Vivi, and Gloria—The beautiful Greek aunts, along with the only boy, handsome Uncle Harry (and let's never forget Uncle Stan!), who helped

MaryLou raise Heath to be the incredible person he was. He learned so much about being a thoughtful, loyal man who treated women well because he grew up surrounded by all of you ladies with your different, but dynamic, personalities. Of course, ten people sharing one bathroom under one roof for years also probably taught him a lot about patience! I love you all!

Jeff Denney, Travis Hadley, Cody Krogh, PK Ramsey— To the dads who stepped up when Heath left us so unexpectedly. You were like brothers to him, and even though you've had your own grief to deal with, you have been there repeatedly for my kids and me. I'm so grateful for each of you, my "backup husbands!" Thank you for all you've done to keep this mom and her house, cars, boats, and kids finely tuned and taken care of!

(P.S. Jeffrey—Uncle Jeff, my brother from another mother—your continued love and support over the years never goes unnoticed! Thank you for loaning me your wife Laurie to be my sidekick whenever I need her!)

Kim Hadley, the Thelma to my Louise, my rock 'n' roll soul sister—Thank you for the many years of incredible friendship! Who knew that running into you when the boys were in preschool would lead us (and our families) to all the adventures we've had together? I'm so grateful for our sisterhood and appreciate you reviewing this book for me more than you know. Love you!

Jared Smith (Smack)—Thank you for being Heath's lifelong friend. I know it's not the same without him here. And I know he'll wait for you and pick up right where you left off, likely ready for some snow skiing in the sky. I am so sorry for your loss. Never forget that the McHenrys love you!

The Hamiltons and the Stepps—Thank you for being with my husband on his last day on Earth. Heath couldn't have picked a better group to spend his final hours with. I can only imagine how difficult this has been for your families, especially the littlest ones, to process that day and his untimely departure. Please know that my kids, YiaYia, and I are extremely grateful to you all for your love and support, even while you had to handle your own grief. We love you all!

Scott Lisle—You were always one of Heath's dearest friends, as well as colleague and confidante. Thank you for your love and guidance of all things financial and family since Heath's passing. It helps to know that when I need an extra ear, I can call you and trust that you have our family's best interest at heart. All the love to you, Liz, and the boys!

To my Spokane widow warriors—Lori, Shana, Elena, Stephanie, Lynette, Allisyn, Leann, Natalie, and my Instagram widow bestie, Ona—I'm so proud of us. And our husbands would be, too. Love you all!

Jake Kelfer—Your ability to light up a room is invaluable! The way you cheer others on and create such an inviting space at your writer's workshop—free of drama and judgment—is inspiring. Your passion for helping others, your spot-on suggestions, and your off-the-charts enthusiasm gave me the confidence and boost I needed to embark on this book journey. I'm forever grateful! Let's gooooo!

Caitlin Hatzenbuhler—Thank you for being my accountability partner, along with Tanya. I'm excited for your book to reach all the moms who need to hear your wisdom!

MT, Adrienne, Mikey, Carly—Thank you for helping me put my thoughts to words, for believing in me and my message, and for giving me so much support during this process. I am indebted to you and the whole BIB crew!

About The Author

Laurie Denney Photography, 2024

Kelsy McHenry is a mother of three, widow to Heath, and founder of BLOOM *with Kelsy*. She knows firsthand the challenges of balancing family and work, as well as navigating life as a single parent while struggling with deep loss. Through her book writing, *Mama's Gotta BLOOM* podcast, and events focused on inspiring women, Kelsy aims to motivate and encourage moms, especially, to pursue their goals and dreams despite self-doubt, obstacles, or setbacks. Her social media followers have been inspired by her journey and continue to be uplifted by her as she has shared her ups and downs with complete honesty and transparency. In her next chapter, Kelsy looks forward to more coffee, wine, and adventures with her family and friends.

Made in United States
Troutdale, OR
11/25/2024

25256026R00151